Christian Social Ethics
in a Global Era

Christian Social Ethics in a Global Era

Max L. Stackhouse
Peter L. Berger
Dennis P. McCann
M. Douglas Meeks

ABINGDON PRESS STUDIES IN
CHRISTIAN ETHICS AND ECONOMIC LIFE #1

Abingdon Press
Nashville

Library of Congress Cataloging-in-Publication Data

Christian social ethics in a global era / Max L. Stackhouse . . . [et al.].
    p.   cm. — (Abingdon Press studies in Christian ethics and economic life; #1)
    Includes bibliographic references.
    ISBN 0-687-00335-0 (alk. paper)
    1. Christian ethics. 2. Sociology, Christian. 3. Social ethics.
I. Stackhouse, Max L. II. Series.
BJ1251.C5241995
241—dc2095-36884

Unless otherwise noted, all Scripture quotations are from the New Revised Standard Version Bible, copyright © 1989 by the Division of Christian Education of the National Council of the Churches of Christ in the USA. Used by permission.

The quotations on pp. 99 and 102–3 are from *Sources of Indian Tradition*, trans. William Theodore DeBary, copyright © 1958 by Columbia University Press. Reprinted by permission of the publisher.

This book is printed on acid-free, recycled paper.

95 96 97 98 99 00 01 02 03 04 — 10 9 8 7 6 5 4 3 2 1

Manufactured in the United States of America

Contents

Preface

This series is written to aid in the reconstruction of Christian Ethics as it bears on economic life in our increasingly global era. Reconstruction is necessary because much of the analysis used by theologians and pastors to think about economic life in the past few decades is socially and theologically suspect.

It is not only political scientists who failed to predict the collapse of Eastern Europe by failing to read the signs of the times. Nor was it only economists who argued for massive loans by private banks to doubtful governments and did not foresee the consequences of these debts. Nor can we say it was only sociologists who denied the evidence of religious resurgence around the world because they believed that modernization would secularize everyone, or only anthropologists who argued that religion is an aspect of culture and every culture's ethic is equal to every other one, or only politicians who began to see all issues only in terms of power analysis. It was not even only philosophers and literary critics who began to deconstruct every normative claim. These all contributed to the demoralization of intellectual and religious life, to a vacuity in social ethics; but, it must be said, it was also the theologians and pastors.

In conferences on the implications of the Fall of the Wall sponsored by the Lilly Endowment, one hosted by Trotz Rendtorff in Munich and the other by Peter Berger in Boston, it became obvious that ideological commitments had obscured for many the deeper social and ethical forces, as well as many biblical and theological motifs, over the past several decades. It is not that no contribution to the future was made in these decades. Some evil was undone; some good was done. Many colonial, racist, and sexist structures were challenged if not fully banished, and many people were exposed to new possibilities. But many views of what brought these about, and many of the theologies and social theories which advocates use to guide the present toward the future are thin, false, confused, or perilous. They cannot help construct the moral fabric for a global society.

We are closer to Ezra and Nehemiah, rebuilding the city on the base of the past, or the early church, engaging and reshaping a cosmopolitan culture, than we are to the Exodus, the Conquest, the Apocalypse, or the New Jerusalem. The prophetic task today is boldly to reconstruct social ethics under insecure and ambiguous conditions, while confessing our sins and seeking to be socially realistic, intellectually cogent, and theologically faithful.

To reform ethics, we offer a series of volumes, exploring the following hypotheses, recognizing that not everyone agrees:

- We face the prospect of a worldwide, multicultural society in which democratic, constitutional polities, human rights, ethnic interests, nationalist forces, media images, and corporate capitalist forces will be influential—and in conflict, needing ethical guidance.

- Economic forces are largely driving these developments and are themselves substantially driven by materialistic motivations, but they are also shaped by and subject to social, cultural, and spiritual influences, even if these are presently confused, inarticulate, or questionable.

- Religion invariably shapes a society's cultural and spiritual values; thus, no area of social life is purely secular, but since religion exists in the midst of social realities, it makes a great deal of difference what religion is present and how it relates to social realities.

- Economic life, as a peculiar mix of calculated interest, sociopolitical formation, and religio-ethical commitment, stands as a key test as to whether the future will be a blessing or a curse to humanity.

- Theological understandings of the Bible and the classic tradition, in a reconstructive dialogue with the social and human sciences, can correct religious errors, contribute to the understanding of social and economic life, and provide a Christian Ethic to guide the emerging world civilization.

Such issues will be pursued by the method of "apologetic dialogue." "Apologetics" is often contrasted to "dogmatics," which seeks to set forth the doctrinal teaching of the church on its own terms. Dogmatics has its important place, and will often serve as a resource to our efforts. But apologetics seeks to show when, where, and how Christian faith and ethics are intellectually and morally valid. Since many do not know of, hold to, or care about dogmatic matters as they bear on social and economic life, we have to show the significance of theology in public discourse.

We do this in a dialogical setting and for the dialogical settings of teaching and learning. Our editorial board gathers twice a year for discussion, and each volume will have three or more perspectives on its topic. The Board and all contributors are Christian, and all have studied the relationship of Christian ethics to economic life. We come from several backgrounds and traditions—Ecumenical, Evangelical, and Roman Catholic. Most are Protestant. We represent several fields of study. Every position is not present. No one is flatly libertarian, humanist, liberationist, or fundamentalist. We suspect that these views tend to be reductionistic, dishonest, and unfaithful. Yet, we also suspect that each of these views poses a question that must be answered: What preserves individual dignity? What place do we give to humanist values? What serves the poor and the oppressed? And what is fundamental in faith and morals?

We are believers seeking to identify the ethics for economic reconstruction, less like talk shows or party platforms to vent opinion or gain power, than like seminars or discussion groups where people study important matters from different angles, try to plumb deeper, seek a truer view, and find a better way for the common life. We invite all who will to join us.

Future Volumes in Preparation

The Business Corporation and Productive Justice
David Krueger, with Donald W. Shriver, Jr., and Laura Nash

Ecotheology, Creation, and Nature
Thomas Derr, with James A. Nash and Richard John Neuhaus

Callings, Roles, and Relationships: Women and Men in Business
Shirley Roels, with Paul Camenish and Barbara Andolsen

Other volumes under discussion, to be announced.

Chapter 1

Christian Social Ethics in a Global Era: Reforming Protestant Views

Max L. Stackhouse

If the Christian traditions that have shaped so much of the spiritual and social life of our contemporary world are not to fade into oblivion, bringing an utter collapse of civil society, a renewal of Christian ethics as it bears on economic life is necessary. At present, the churches speak with a divided voice where they are not silent, boring, or ideological. The mass media portray religious values as reactionary. Economic and political leadership think church leaders are out of touch or wildly utopian. And academia is contemptuous of, where not blind to, the relation of theology to social issues.

The condescension, suspicion, and neglect are not entirely without justification. The Roman Catholic Church at present seems bent upon embracing the presuppositions and effects of the modernization it so long opposed, while calling on contemporary societies to share its assumptions and fruits with the poor and the oppressed, whom its cultural embrace of feudalism helped keep that way. At the same time, many Pentecostals and Fundamentalists around the world seem to be generating a raw new version of the "Protestant Ethic." It transforms the families of those whom everyone thought would join "base communities" in the tradition of liberation theology into micro-entrepreneurial firms, but it does so in ways that are only partly distinguishable from what some have identified as a "Confucian Ethic" in Pacific rim countries, now bringing development to Asia. It also remains mostly devoid of a systematic theology of social, political, or economic ethics.

Meanwhile, the Orthodox traditions of the East seem lost in the massive transition from communism to the rather brutal forms of mafia capitalism that have swept Eastern Europe; their historic alliances with czarist political economics did not equip them for the kind of society into which they have been plunged. And those traditions rooted in the Protestant Reformation seem today particularly incapable of speaking clearly to the new, post-socialist, global situation we face.[1] Some echo Luther's "Two Kingdom" teachings in a way that divides matters of theology from those of society. Other parts of Protestantism echo the Anglican traditions that tended toward Erastianism—the subordination of religion and economics to national sovereignty. And still others recapitulate a sectarian heritage that resists culture altogether, especially if "capitalist values" or the use of coercive force in politics is involved.

Nevertheless, the wider Christian view, Catholic, Orthodox, Reformed, and Evangelical, holds important, even indispensable, resources for the renewal of the churches and thereby of souls and civilization. If that is so, as I believe it to be, the burden of proof is upon Christian leaders. Not only do the secular world and every alternative religious tradition not believe in these religious resources, neither do many Christian pastors and teachers today.

Assessing the decline of "mainline" religion has, to be sure, become something of a cottage industry among ministers, sociologists of religion, and theological commentators. It is not my purpose here to engage in yet another such assessment, for several compelling accounts of the demographic and spiritual changes that have reduced the number, influence, and vitality of these churches by approximately one-third in one generation already exist. Many studies contain helpful suggestions as to how worship, pastoral care, preaching, and teaching can be reinvigorated. However, few of these studies specifically treat the nature or character of the social witness that these churches could make in view of the massive transformations that are changing the structures of the common life at both local and global levels. In fact, a number of the critics of present church trends claim that many of the difficulties of the churches come from the fact that they are already too focused on social questions.

Too Much Social Focus?

The truth of such a charge is highly doubtful. With the exception of various proclamations that do stir debate in the press, most believers and most churches do not spend much of their time, energy, or money attempting to interpret or address the social realities of our day in a theologically grounded way. It is also not clear that these traditions would be strengthened by reducing their social witness; and it could demoralize them.

The Catholic tradition of the pre-Reformation period forged much that is central to Western civilization, and that has been partly recovered and recast in the Social Encyclicals from Leo XIII to John Paul II in this century. The heirs of the Reformation—from Luther, Calvin, and Zwingli through the Presbyterians, Congregationalists, Episcopalians, Methodists, and Baptists, to the twentieth-century advocates of the Social Gospel, Christian realism, civil rights, modern ecumenical, and some Evangelical movements—extended and refined that classic tradition, specifically on social and economic questions. They would betray their faith if they did not constantly renew their efforts to articulate a public theology that is able to guide the church, to shape the structures of civilization, and to call persons to participation in the ongoing institutions that sustain the common life in just and compassionate societies.

It is not true that the Gospel is irrelevant to these issues or that these issues are irrelevant to the Gospel. On the one hand, a case can be made that when the Gospel is viewed as irrelevant to these issues, it stops being the Gospel and becomes simply irrelevant. It is a key function of theology as understood in the classic traditions to provide the basic framework whereby humanity can participate in the formation, and the perennial reformation, of both church and society. No theology can long endure that does not relate the truth it discloses to the changing contexts of social existence so that vital communities of worship can shape responsible societies, stable personalities, and enduring civilizations.

On the other hand, every vital theology evokes personal commitment to shape habits and relationships that accord with the best we can know of God's will. It thereby supplies the moral core of what our forebears variously called "virtuous and blessed" or "righteous and sanctifying" engagement in the common life—a far cry from what some treat as only sanctimonious arrogance. Without a deep and personal commitment, churches and societies fall apart as surely as they do when the fabric of the common life decays or remains unformed by moral and spiritual values. Simultaneously, without social support, the moral efforts of persons are frustrated. Then, everything has to be done anew, alone, and from scratch. People become incapable of making wider social contributions.

13

A theology that does not reach into the tissues of the common life through well-structured frameworks for living, as well as through the evocation of personal commitment, is not worth much. What kind of a God would be at the heart of such a theology? What kind of ethical logic or religion would we have if they were entirely disengaged from social, familial, technological, and cultural life? How could we develop legal, educational, medical, and business institutions to mitigate the disorder, ignorance, illness, and poverty that is present in every human society if we did not have communities of commitment calling us to justice and compassion? What sort of a civilization would we have, in other words, if it were it not informed by theology, ethics, and religion, or if it were informed by a theological, ethical, or religious tradition entirely different from the one that has in fact shaped the Western traditions?

My purpose here, then, is not to reduce the emphasis on society or on justice, but to clear some of the intellectual clutter that has accumulated on the ground where important parts of the church stand. Some recent efforts to address issues of justice have been not only misguided, but viciously destructive of human well-being, precisely because they have neglected key theological motifs and turned to secular, neo-pagan, and anti-Christian monisms to define the problems we face.

To spend much time and space on views of our social and economic situation—views that have been widely debated in political and academic circles—may seem repetitive to some. But they have had a distinctive shape and history in religious circles, and the topics to be discussed in the body of this essay are ones that have defined the field of ethics that Christians have sought to till in our time. When one puts the hand to the plow and seeks to cultivate the field in a new season, it is wise to be sure where the fertile ground is and what residues of the winter and stubble from the past threaten to foul our plowshares.

What continues to define the furrows of our field as we try to think about the future are hopes for a modified, democratic social-ism; theories of liberation; concerns about the decline of the family, the rise of the corporation, and the power of the media; apparent triumphs by neo-liberals and neo-conservatives; an ideology of the "Third World"; and a "Green" agenda. These do not all fit together in a convenient package, but they continue to dominate religious and ethical thinking about economic life today. Around these topics, there is much clutter that cannot be sorted by the conventional labels of "liberal" and "conservative," especially where those tags block the priority of theological and ethical renewal.

Ideas have consequences. Subtly bad ideas are the most devastating: they hold the attention longer, gain trust sooner, evoke deeper loyalty, and appeal to wider constituencies than blatantly foolish ones. We should be reminded that demons, in the theological tradition, are fallen angels. Thus, as we sort each of these issues, turn toward planting, and look to a new harvest, the purpose will be to restore what is valuable and to relegate what is distorted to the fires.

Facing Socialist Confusions

For a century, at least, socialism has presented itself as on the side of the angels: on the side of the progressives, the radicals, and the moral activists and intellectuals who challenge the conventional approval of constitutional democracy, bourgeois lifestyles, and corporate capitalism. However, in both its national socialist and its proletarian socialist forms, it has proven to be regressive, superficial, demonically destructive of morality, and incapable of developing a viable, urbane lifestyle. Few religious leaders today openly advocate any form of socialism; but their opposition to the world emerging on the far side of its collapse echoes of their devotion to its values.[2]

I am well aware that putting the matter this directly will raise the defenses of many whom I ultimately hope to persuade. Not a few teachers and preachers have spent much time and energy trying to get students and parishioners to overcome their "enemy-image" of everyone on the left end of the conventional spectrum, to recognize that the socialist options and programs are varied and neither substitutes for nor prologues to communism, and to keep in mind that capitalist systems are not beyond criticism and reform. They recoil from general suggestions that socialism is problematic. At least, they hold, it is a useful critic or corrective of the excesses of capitalism, even if it too is subject to criticism as a system. But they have not followed the best of socialist advice: to engage in the concrete analysis of real economic and political life as it has continued to develop. Thus, the categories of analysis that they use are freighted with lenses that are outdated and lopsided, and they confuse church and society with their rhetoric. Some need, thus, to have an alternative stated in strong terms to wake them out of their dogmatic slumbers. Some will never be able to rethink the issues, and we must regretfully leave them behind as period pieces who contributed in their day, reaching instead to the new generation who can overcome their confusions.

The confusion is especially pronounced in discussions about the nature and character of economic life, a much broader concept than economics proper, since it takes historical, social, familial, political, cultural, and ethical factors into account. Although economics always takes place in the context of both a socio-historical context and certain general assumptions about culture and nature (assumptions that are inevitably informed by religion), the science of economics tries its best to blot out those factors, by calling them "externalities," or "preferences." The exclusion of these factors makes certain data more manageable; but precisely these same exclusions and hidden assumptions distort our sense of the fullness of economic life. In fact, the assumptions about social forces, human motives, cultural values, moral principles, ethical purposes, and the power of religion are ignored by some economic theories, and distorted by others. Because the widespread understanding of Adam Smith ignored these, many religious leaders turned to widespread views of Karl Marx, which distorted them.

We can see this point in other fields. Jurisprudence may be critical for medical practice, but it is not a sufficient guide in the actual care of patients, and its presumptions can actually distort that care. Architecture is necessary in building a house, but it tells us little about making a home and can make family life difficult if it does not get the dynamics in a culture right. So, economics may do technical things well, but may lead to distortions of life if it does not see the religious, ethical, and social dynamics behind the numbers.

If these confusions are not debated and, where appropriate, corrected, Christianity will, and should, fade into enclaves of alienated sectarianism. Contemporary economic life will become as soulless as the political economy of the Soviet Union. But if the problems are acknowledged, debated and corrected, it becomes possible to foresee a renewal of both Christian ethics and of contemporary economic morality. To sort these confusions, of course, an alternative must be set forth as well as a critique. This is the larger purpose of this volume, and of this series of volumes—to help inaugurate a reconstruction of Christian Ethics in and for the churches.

A full reformation of the Christian traditions would, among other things, demand a fresh engagement with the great world religions, and, even more, a revitalization of worship, stewardship, religious education, engagement with the arts, and pastoral care. Our central focus here, however, is a basic recovery and recasting of a theological approach to social and economic matters in the face of the new conditions we face—conditions, in fact, that the Reformation traditions particularly helped bring into being, but which today are often interpreted without reference to their inherent moral or spiritual realities. These conditions thus have to be seen from points of view that are alert to religious and theological issues.

The work of Protestant Christianity is not over. Yet a new appreciation of and interdependence with Roman Catholicism is also well warranted, for it too has been undergoing reformation. Obviously, many areas remain in dispute, especially areas related to birth control and the role of women in religious leadership, which bear in them deep disputes about the nature of nature, technology, human sexuality, and the family, as other volumes in this series will treat. These traditions are not ready to reunite; but both Protestants and Catholics will fail if the Christian ministry to our age is not revitalized.

Triumph and Tragedy

In the area of social witness, Christianity has a great deal to celebrate. Much that it struggled for in the last centuries has come to pass. In spite of many detours and distortions, the common Catholic tradition shaped a great and complex culture and a rich, dynamic civilization. It is in that context that the Reformation recovered and recast certain key aspects of the biblical tradition that had become obscured, and pressed the main contours of Western civilization away from feudalism toward democracy, from hierarchy toward pluralism, from religiously sanctioned statism toward the separation of church and state, and from a societally alienated spirituality toward a theologically informed laity who could engage historical and material life with ethical competence.

Certainly, Christianity can celebrate the fulfillment of its prayers during the twentieth century. The kaisers and czars who invoked the name of God to crush the independence of the church, populist piety, and democratic movements early in the century are barely noted in history books. The houses of the robber barons, who brought us rapacious forms of early industrialization before plunging us into the Depression, now are retreat centers or condominiums. Fascism was subdued. Imperialistic colonialism was overthrown, although the churches, schools, and hospitals in many parts of the world remain as a legacy of the mission movement that spread with colonialism. National socialism was defeated and communism has collapsed. All these are now toothless lions; they have lost the capacity to savage the earth.

Moreover, human rights and constitutional democracy are more widely recognized around the globe than ever before, in spite of many and persistent violations. We now have more social, legal, and moral constraints on discrimination and violence against ethnic minorities and women than at any time in history, although racism and sexism persist. We must acknowledge that the victims of such abuses have no reason to rejoice—and our work is not done—when their pain is unacknowledged or its causes remain unaddressed by the churches.

At another level, we are now seeing the most massive "build down" of military forces and weaponry ever, as state after state demobilizes soldiers, machinery, nuclear weaponry, and military industries, from Moscow to Washington, Havana to Johannesburg, and New Delhi to Buenos Aires. This is in spite of the fact that the pagan deity Mars still lurks as a tempter in the recesses of conscious-ness, the advocates for redesigning the military for new conditions tell us that it is likely to cost more, and the capacity to build massive weapons of destruction is likely to remain with us for as long as we can imagine a future.

Further, in the life-span of school children, "people power" de-feated Marcos in the Philippines; military regimes in Latin America and Africa relinquished power to civilian, democratic governments; and one-party states from Vietnam to Mozambique to Myanmar to Nicaragua creep toward democratic politics and open economies as they now eagerly solicit international investments. Mandela and deKlerk received the peace prize together; Arafat shook hands with Peres; and Egypt, Syria, and Jordan have signed peace treaties with Israel.

Still more, we face a new international interdependency that invites us into new relationships with our neighbors near and far in spite of the resurgence of ethnic and tribal violence in troubled, bloody corners of the globe. Now, enjoying each other's cuisine, sharing each other's customs, singing each other's songs, producing and buying each other's goods, and even thinking each other's thoughts is more widely possible than ever before. However super-ficial most of this seems most of the time, the multicultural reality of pluralism is a fact of life as well as an educational slogan. Global is what we are and do.

At the same time, Christians are not inclined to euphoria over such things. We know too much about sin. We remind ourselves that grinding poverty remains in many places, that pitiful refugees die in droves as they flee violence and famine, that the heirs of Fascism reappear both as Baathists in the Middle East and as "respectable" parties in the West, that neo-Nazi movements emerge like zombies from the grave, and that ex-Communists become the *nouveau riche* managers of government bureaucracies and new corporations in former Socialist countries. "Multiculturalism" and "pluralism" be-come, in the hands of some, ideologies of relativism against every principle that Christianity ever held.

Nor may we forget the violence of our own history in the Cru-sades and the wars of religion, on the frontier, in slavery and under the banner of a "manifest destiny." In the midst of this emerging global civilization emerging on the brink of a new century, we must surely also remember that many forebears believed that our times would bring us "the Christian Century." We now know it as the century that brought with it not only six hundred thousand deaths at Hiroshima and Nagasaki, but also six million deaths in the Holo-caust and sixteen million deaths in the Gulag. Utopian hopes are chastised by memory into modesty.

Many of these ghastly events were prompted by resistance to constitutional democracy, human rights, and economic corporations independent of state control, all historically defended by (some say essentially generated by) Protestantism. Today, the resistance may be modulated, but it subsides precisely as the Protestant churches that supported these developments suffer decline. It is an open question whether these institutions can be sustained if the basic beliefs that generated them fade in the consciousness of the population and the forms of civil society that supported them cannot reproduce them-selves.

Of Freedom and Holiness

If Protestantism has played its role in the drama of God's history and must now leave center stage, so be it. It was always dependent on the biblical heritage and the Catholic tradition, and it tried to extend and correct the tradition by discerning the fuller implications of the biblical heritage. When that task is accomplished, Protestantism has no distinct contribution. But it is not clear that Protestants should resign themselves to oblivion. We face, indeed, the haunting possibility that contemporary civilization is suffering from the consequences of a certain confusion in our own heritage that we have resolved in the wrong direction in our times, and that we must repair this confusion in ourselves or wreak great damage even as we die.

Protestants are, by nature, protesters. We know that the energies of our own will—and our own virtues, accomplishments, creations, and achievement—do not suffice. Even the most sincere exercise of religious devotion cannot satisfy the deepest hungers of the human heart, cure the egocentric streak that taints every human act of generosity, order our human relationships or prevent the tendency to idolatry that resides in every spiritual attainment.

Protestants know that we must depend ultimately on God and God alone. Justification remains the centerpoint of faith. Thus, over the centuries, we have challenged pretension at every point in church and society—even in our own classic heritage. That led most Protestants to read the Bible in critical ways, and to be very cautious about *sola Scriptura*. The debate over this issue is what divides Protestants from those who have taken the tradition toward Fundamentalism. Further, *sola fide* has not only tempted parts of our tradition to accept absurdities blindly, but it has tempted others to a mere "beliefism," a rejection by many in the churches of the normative importance of doctrine in favor of the observation that everyone has to have some kind of faith, and it really does not make any difference how it is understood, so long as it is sincerely held.

Nevertheless, Protestants have a hard time giving up a full commitment to *sola gratia*, for that is the basis of what is true about the other two major Protestant principles. This is what unites us with Catholic, Orthodox, and Evangelical Christians. Both the common grace that allows all peoples to know something about God, truth, and justice and to resist religious claims that are utter nonsense, and the special grace to which the Scriptures witness under the most intense scrutiny and which well-formed doctrines articulate, render a kind and quality of knowledge that is critical for the well-being of persons, churches, communities, and civilizations.

Protestants, thus, must challenge each other and all conventional authorities, and demand the free social space for God's gracious inspiration, innovation, and transformation. The impulse to challenge pretentious authority is not rooted in some enlightened philosophy that invented critical thinking and thus surpassed all religion; nor is it rooted in an economic or political resentment—however just—that poor and oppressed peoples feel toward the rich and the powerful. The record of critical thinking in religion is more profound than the record of thinking against it; and stories of resentment are matched many times over by stories of ingratiation and imitation. The deeper impulse to critical thinking is found in the prophetic tradition of the Old and New Testaments. That, more than anything else, engenders a drive for liberty that is one of two great themes of the heritage.

But at the center of this freedom we find a second impulse—one that is centered on holiness in the midst of the world. This theme invites us to obedience to the laws, purposes, and callings of God. Protestant Christianity remains an authentic form of the faith only insofar as it holds firmly to the notion that God's grace is manifest not only in the experience of freedom from the tyrannies of arrogance, distrust, pain and sin, but also in the experience of a demand to live by a divine righteousness that rules over the whole universe: an ultimate purpose that guides destiny, a calling to use the talents that are given us to participate responsibly in the formation and sustaining of the common life. In other words, the grace of freedom has a *raison d'être*—holiness. Protest on behalf of freedom is only half of what Protestantism, at its best, has to offer.

It is only in obedience to holiness (what some call discipleship, sanctification, or the "imitation of Christ") that we find the patterns of meaning behind the reality of freedom. In the laws of God we see a principle of order that prevents chaos and offers to freedom a framework of justice and truth-telling. In the purposes of God, we are drawn toward constructive possibilities that are not yet fully actual, a vision that beacons and beckons us into creative action, and the good beyond the immediately practical. And in the callings of God, we find those networks of mutually accountable associations and relationships that give social form to the gifts, crafts, talents, and professions by which the covenants of civilization are constantly renewed.

The freedom that Protestantism affirms and defends is thus misunderstood if it is seen as merely the freedom of the self to be itself. Protestantism places the freedom of the self under an authority that is beyond the self, and beyond any other human self. No one can properly dominate another; neither is a mature self one who entirely rules itself and refuses to submit itself to a law, purpose, or calling beyond itself.

It is one of the deepest convictions of the Protestant Reformation, in accord with the whole Christian tradition, that the self is not complete in isolation, but only in a relationship that confers and confirms its meaning—and no relationship ultimately does that except a relationship to God. At its deeper levels the human self, and liberty itself, and hence every enjoyment of a free society—from a freely chosen marriage partner, to a free press, to a free market system—stands under the judgment of a holiness that is beyond the freedom. The temptations to hegemony, to heteronomy, to domination, exploitation, manipulation, and deception, are so many and so frequent in human affairs that Protestantism has often become closely tied to radical demands for liberty that celebrate the human self itself. It is not difficult to see why Protestantism became allied, in various times and places, with parts of the Renaissance and the Enlightenment, or with Romanticism and with liberal social protest movements. All of these fostered, each in a distinctive way, freedom and autonomy—sometimes for groups, sometimes for individuals. And Protestantism, where it was faithful to itself, properly defended these values against the onslaughts of tyranny and oppression that are frequent in social history.

Yet Protestantism centers its defense of individual and group freedom in different places than do these movements. It understands the human self as most fully developed when it is in full, conscious relationship to God, and thus empowered to take on the discipline of living in covenanted relationships with others. Protestants treasure each person, for each soul has the capacity to become related to God. By the grace of God, each person is made in the image of God; through the Holy Spirit, every person is invited into a relationship with God. This redemptive relation between the human person and God, and between persons (a relation which is more often one of estrangement than of communion, is what Christians know is possible through Christ. That is the core of the Christian confidence that love ordered by justice is the central ethical meaning of holiness. It drives all touched by it into bonded associations of disciplined service.

22

Protestantism therefore joins other advocates of freedom so that the liberty to reform (and to point out the necessity of reform in all human relationships) may be defended. And it ever seeks more nearly to approximate and nurture the possibility of holy relationships that bring the human into conjunction with the divine, and to embody that relationship in every aspect of life. It would not be false to say that Protestantism is always meddling in things beyond religion if it were true that there are areas of life that are and ought to be beyond the reign of God. But there are no such areas. Every area of life, including economics, is seen by Protestants as subject to the criteria of freedom and holiness, of justice and love.

Freedom, Holiness, and Worldliness

Both justice and love, however, have structures. They are not the flow of primal energy, like adolescent hormones, gushing aimlessly without order or focus, taking new liberties. Yet, in our times, the prophetic Protestant demand for freedom has become detached from a sense of holiness and attached to several understandings of the human condition that undermine both freedom and holiness. For many in the ecumenical Protestant churches, the notion of freedom, human or divine, has been largely absorbed into post- or anti-theological understandings. This is partly because these have come to dominate modern secular thought, and active participants are often among the best educated church members in the world. But these movements have also cultivated a number of intellectual and spiritual impulses that many Protestants recognize as allies.

Among these allies, the idea of holiness seems quaint. We are humans, and there are few saints among us, they say. Besides, it seems so much more interesting to realize our humanness than to aspire to something beyond the bounds of ordinariness. After all, was it not Protestantism that took piety and spiritual discipline out of the monasteries and into daily life? And are not priests and nuns belatedly following Protestants into marriage and worldly callings, in spite of magisterial opposition? Believers of many kinds today introduce democratic polities into their congregations and become involved in political movements on religious grounds, and religious leaders in many traditions use corporate, economic, and technological methods of management, accounting, market analysis, and goal-setting.

23

But, of course, that is just the point. Protestantism did not reject holiness; it simply discerned its practical locus to be at once more transcendent and more materially incarnate than was previously thought. The pure holiness of God is to be found in, and only in, God, who is other than, above, and beyond the world. But since the laws, purposes, and callings of God have been most fully disclosed in the one who is fully human as well as fully God, Jesus Christ, they are to be obeyed, pursued, and practiced precisely in the midst of the common life: in marriage, the law court, the university, politics, and the market place. That is why an ordered freedom is demanded in the institutions of the common life, so that the relative approximations to holiness possible in history may be actualized on earth as they are in heaven—not so that heaven can be lowered and we, being human, can settle into the moral and spiritual mediocrity to which we tend.

In the struggles for liberty, Protestants have been allied with the Renaissance, Enlightenment, Romanticism, liberalism, and liberation movements in successive periods of Western history. Protestants today are not inclined to say that what these alliances affirmed, in their defense of freedom and autonomy—sometimes for individuals, sometimes for peoples or nations—is false or worthless or evil, as many anti-modernists and postmodernists today claim. Instead, Protestants joined these struggles because they opposed forces that both denied freedom and crushed genuine impulses toward personal or social holiness. Yet those alliances explain why many Protestant churches are often called "liberal." The term is borne with pride by many Protestants against obscurantists and reactionaries of all kinds.

Protestants view their faith as largely commensurate, and necessarily in dialogue, with the best of literary, historical, and scientific thought. The liberal arts are companions, not enemies. Further, those Protestants who advocated for political life the freedom of religion, speech and assembly, the necessity of the limited state, and the rights of minorities have persuaded their fellow believers who earlier had reservations about these points. Most Protestants agree with those philosophical traditions that hold that it is possible to know something about justice without knowing about Jesus Christ; and thus they see cooperation between Christians and humanists, or Christians and adherents of other faiths, as an open option (although they say that this is due to "common grace" or "general revelation" rather than to "natural law," for the latter implies that we can know the right and the good entirely without God).

The critics of such Protestants, however, sometimes raise the question as to which is the substantive noun and which is the qualifying adjective when the terms "liberal" and "Christian" appear in the same phrase. Indeed, both more "conservative" Christians and more "radical" humanists wonder why "Christian liberals" bother to be religious: nothing, say these critics, makes their ethics or their public stands distinctive. Some of that wonder is due to ignorance of the ways in which historic Protestantism integrated faith and reason in its view of revelation, its efforts to preach and teach persuasively, and its joining of descriptive and normative modes of discourse in pastoral work. But on the question of morality, the critics may have a point: the definition of freedom in parts of "liberal Protestantism" has become severed from its classical commitment to holiness, to obedience to the laws and purposes and callings of God. Calls for freedom thus tempt Protestantism to drift with the currents, with no clearer focus for reform or commitment than the ever-increased demand for more liberty.

The Protestant drive for freedom, because it was anchored in the holiness of God's laws, purposes, and callings, stabilized the implicit anarchy present in the demand for freedom found among its secular allies; together this marriage of freedom and holiness played a decisive role in human history in confrontations with feudalism, the "divine right of kings," patriarchal domination, colonialism, and a host of totalitarian or authoritarian systems, historic and contemporary.

But it is doubtful that this part of our witness can address the central question we now face: what can—and what ought to—guide the churches, and thus human personalities and human societies, in our new geoeconomic world, a world that is increasingly free, thanks in large part to the combined force of Protestantism and its secular allies who also struggled for liberty? The question is especially difficult since it seems to some that Protestantism has so displaced its inner drive to holiness by its effort to establish freedom without reference to God's laws, purposes, and callings that it has allowed freedom to become the highest, indeed the only, value. A few modern theologians even accent "the freedom of God" as a central doctrine, as if both God's character and God's relationship to the world had no measure of order, justice, and constancy.

We may rejoice that Protestantism and its allies have been sufficiently effective that great parts of the world live in more and more open, liberal societies. But if it proves to be so that the most pronounced forms of tyranny and oppression are less threatening, the question before humanity is altered. The central question is not how to get more freedom, but what to do morally, spiritually, socially, and economically with the freedom at hand.

Three Transformations

It is possible that contemporary humanity has, in remarkable, unexpected, and perhaps even miraculous ways, escaped for at least a time the perils of Pharaoh, and has come to a place where the instruments of military power are rendered as impotent as chariots trying to charge through a marsh. But we may also be in a moral and spiritual wilderness where the guiding patterns of life are not clear, where some only remember the securities of the past while others only anticipate a utopian promised land. In the confusions of this situation, we find at least three areas where chaos seduces freedom, tempting it to anomie, purposelessness, and the nihilism of an all-pervasive hermeneutics of suspicion: family and local community life, international corporate and commercial life, and high-tech electronic communications. These deeply influence civil society and hence economic life, and each prompts theological analysis and evokes calls for ethical reformation.

To treat economic life in terms of the structures of civil society that are under challenge accords with several great traditions of social philosophy deriving from the Reformation. Here, the common life is understood as constituted by a series of necessary institutional arrangements which are always and everywhere required, although they can be structured in a variety of ways. Early Protestant forebears spoke of the "orders of creation." Later heirs of the Reformers wrote of the various "departments of life," or "spheres of relative sovereignty" or "mandates" whereby, in God's providential grace, civility and culture are maintained. Today we are more inclined to speak of various "sectors" of society. This usage, however, also points to a pluralistic civil society constituted by an association of sub-societies, each having its own integrity, yet all forming an open system that serves its members and the whole of civilization.

A key feature of this social theory is its self-conscious distinction from all philosophies that see politics as the overarching and integrating reality of life, to which all other parts of society, including religion, are subsidiary. This view can be found in the ancient Greek *polis*, in the Roman republic, and in many Christian celebrations of King David, the Emperor Constantine, and the Holy Roman Empire. It appears in radical form in modern doctrines of the sovereignty of the nation-state. The Reformed traditions have been sometimes tempted to adopt this general theory, but it leads to totalitarianism, both left and right, as well as to theocracies and caeseropapist domination. The inner convictions of the Reformation (and, Protestants believe, of the Bible) press in the other direction.

The deeper presuppositions of Protestantism see society as prior to politics. Centered in the life of faith, but taking shape in the formation of the family, the community, the school, the arts, and the economy, as well as the government, it treats government as but one of the several malleable arenas or sectors of practical human association. Civil society, thus, can be seen as a wider arena, where church members participate in forming the potentially covenanted groups of the common life, each one having a vocation into which the others ought not unduly intrude, but all subject to influence by a religiously informed social ethics able to carry beyond the church gathered in worship.

This society of interacting associations now appears to be in disarray. Indeed, it is a rock-hard and barren place for some, and a lush and manna-laden wilderness for others, into which contemporary life is thrust. It is a wilderness that cannot be tamed by governmental action alone, for key elements of these various and necessary associations that constitute civil society are subject to moral and spiritual guidance that cannot and ought not be controlled by government, although they can and must be supported by strategic political policies. In any case, if these vital associations are not healthy and vibrant, crises will compound and perpetuate difficulties for the next generation.

It simply is not the case that civil society can remain healthy if family life dies, if schools decay, the arts degenerate, and businesses close. This happens not only when vulnerable populations are caught in the cross-fire of economic "creative destruction"; but it is intensified when churches fail to nourish the values, the commitment, and the framework of organization by which these can be sustained. When that is lost, all that remains is control by the police and dole by the social workers. They are surely necessary, but to have only police would be unjust, only social workers would be ineffective. Yet, we cannot expect them alone or together to form or reform souls or societies.

Family

It is clear to all but the most ideological of observers that our problems in civil society have been accompanied by what is widely discussed as "family breakdown." Certainly, with higher percentages of broken families we have seen a range of social problems: single parents—mostly women—left with the huge responsibility both for nurture and economic support of their children; non-custodial parents often absent from their children or disconnected from their responsibilities; and children left without the support they need to thrive in school and prepare for adult relationships. The role of families as a primal source of stability and enduring roots in a community has been diminished, resulting, for many, in alienation from church, school, party, and job—all those institutions by which a community, a town, or a city is held together as a civil society. It is not at all clear that public programs can repair the damage or replace what is lost in people's lives.

A number of long-term transformations beyond the control of government have surely affected family life as well. Key features of family life are shaped by both technological and value shifts. The household is, for example, no longer an indispensable locus of production in advanced economies and is losing its role as a producing unit in developing economies. First, the father's presence became less necessary—he was no longer needed to hunt or fish; to plow, reap, and store the grain; or to raise, tend, and butcher the cattle. In fact, he could do better if he went to the city to work in a factory or an office. Leaving the wife and kids behind became frequent.

Then the mother—no longer required to gather fuel and tend the garden; to milk cows and gather eggs; to cook, can, and freeze the food; or to wash the dishes—found that what took grandmother all week to do could be done by machines in half a day. Yet the fact that household management remained her responsibility seemed unduly sex-stereotyped, and she resented being cast as the one to do it. She too could choose to go to work outside the home: for some in two-parent families, this was an opportunity to increase the family income or to use her talents in new ways. For other women, it was a necessary move, to support themselves and their children.

Nor was either father or mother seen as much needed for the education of their children. For one thing, their skills would be outdated by the time the youngsters needed them. For another, the bus could take them to nursery school, kindergarten, grammar school, and, in some places, two decades of education complete with food service, housekeeping, and guidance counselors. For some time, of course, children—especially in the West—have been less decisive for labor or as protection against old age and disability, but they have had to seek increased levels of formal training to do well in the changing economy. On such points one can either say that such education, once the prerogative of the aristocracy, has become expected by the middle classes and required, at a minimum level, by law for all—education that removes one substantially from parental influence. In any case, the economic support systems that held the "traditional" family together have been weakened by technological and value changes.

Such developments segregated the household from economic necessity. Some tax policies even make it disadvantageous to be married, since government policy increasingly treats all persons as individuals regardless of familial status. The disappearance of the family farm in North America (now less than 2 percent of the population lives on such farms) and the decline of the family business or shop (still a vast number of small firms, but less than 20 percent of the whole economy) are only obvious signals of a trend that can now be seen everywhere in the world. In spite of the fact that people live longer, report happier lives, have better jobs, higher income levels and fewer difficulties with neighbors, friends and the law when they live in stable families, many people experience the formation of a traditional family as an option—something not required for living rightly or well. For others, a stable family seems an unattainable goal, with few viable models.

Viewed in terms of its impact on economic life, the family has become essentially a unit of consumption. Individuals interact sexually, emotionally, and recreationally in the family, and often prize the satisfactions of family life more highly than any other activity. Where these interactions are not satisfying, members go elsewhere to find what they need. Relationships increasingly become serial and temporary. Today, half of new marriages end in divorce or eventually take on all sorts of blended forms (although serial marriages distort the figures significantly).

What is not clear is how much of this shift can be said to be rooted in value changes. We know that technology made possible an increased economic independence of women, and that this has made a great difference in family life; but we do not know how much of this is influenced by cultural values. Nor can we clearly pinpoint the causes of some men ignoring their responsibilities as fathers, or the inability of some to sustain equal marriages with strong, independent women. We know that the negative stigma of out-of-marriage birth has declined, but we do not know all the reasons for the explosion of single parent families. What seems likely is that the drive for individual liberty has not only influenced all of these, but also how we weigh the responsibility to spouse and children relative to other values, and how we understand the true nature of the self.

Ironically, it was the Reformed tradition, and within that Puritanism (for all the residues of patriarchy that it preserved), that pressed for the recognition of the holiness of sexuality, for the necessity of a new equality between male and female in marriage, and for the view that marriage, not celibacy, was what most approximated the laws, purposes, and callings of God. In old Puritan New England, it was illegal to live alone. A companionate marriage bound together by a freely agreed covenant of love shaped not only the wedding services of modernity, but cultural hopes for a relationship of free and mutual accountability. The earlier vows called for a discipline "for better or for worse, for richer or for poorer, in sickness and in health," in which partners were to submit themselves to each other under God's law, for Godly purposes, and to fulfill their callings in freedom and delight so long as both shall live. In many Protestant churches today, couples write their own services of commitment, divorce is fully accepted, and some advise pre-nuptial agreements to anticipate economic settlement when divorce comes.

It is not at all clear that the larger call to holiness is being set forth in a compelling way in modern life, or that people know what is at stake if the issue is raised. Many of the traditional roles that were assigned to men and women are obviously obsolete and many were so laden with stereotyped images that they were oppressive. Protestants have acknowledged that abusive and violent marriages are false covenants that need not be endured passively. But it is also clear that the current lacerations of mind and soul found in sexual and generational relationships cannot be easily mitigated or healed without moral regeneration, that the children of the next generation cannot be prepared for responsibility and maturity without new arrangements for a stable family environment, and that neither civil society in general nor economic life in particular can flourish, without some basic regrounding and reconstruction of family life.

Corporations

In the new world of transnational interactions, we find a second institution that is largely independent of the state, but decisive for the civil society. New patterns of communications, finance, technology and trade, as well as new competition for capital and jobs, make it more difficult for any government to manage economic matters. It has been recognized for some time that the transnational corporation had escaped the control of any particular political system; today we find governments competing with one another as to which one can provide the least controlled environment, in order to induce transnationals to come.

Further, highly mobile networks of corporations are creating flexible and interactive systems of production and distribution. They cater to rapidly changing tastes and felt needs, even as they promote ever increasing levels of desire for consumer goods. These transformations of civil society, which some experience as destruction at local levels and which others see as geoeconomic reconstruction at international levels, also renders some people functionally useless in the face of forces they do not understand and cannot control. At least in the short run, it makes the near poor, the "working poor," more vulnerable, even if it promises to bring higher percentages of the world's populations into the middle classes in the long run.

The global market within which the corporation operates puts more people in competition with workers internationally, and reduces the willingness of governments to regulate labor and ecological practices or to raise taxes for social services in each country, lest that make the national economy less competitive or make corporations more inclined to move elsewhere. Even more, it invites further automation for a range of jobs and encourages increased technology to improve productivity, a fact that makes whole categories of labor at least temporarily dispensable. Yet these same realities make more goods available to more people, and raise the standards of living wherever they go so dramatically, that no political leader who does

31

not seek to attract, keep and support corporations in a global market can hope to be elected in a democratic country.

It does little good, and it is likely false prophecy, to rail against the transnationals and "the globalization of the market" as if these were unambiguously evil. There is little doubt that corporations have at times exploited workers, bought governments, defied the law, threatened the environment, and bilked consumers. We should have no illusions about the fact that they will try to do so again in environments where the social and political controls for complex, powerful economic organizations are weak or subject to easy corruption. I shall say more about this later.

But it is also the case that the modern corporations have generated more wealth for larger percentages of the world's population, transferred more technology to underdeveloped peoples, and provided more leverage against totalitarian regimes than any other arrangement. Indeed, every other organizational instrument yet invented to enhance production and wealth—the *latifundia*, partnership, fief, manor, plantation, caste, Tong, government bureaucracy, etc.—has attempted to do these same things, but without producing wealth as efficiently, and without transferring technology or challenging totalitarian regimes. Indeed, they frequently are so tied to familial or political institutions that every economic transaction has sexual or coercive implications, and every sexual and political action becomes a matter of economic extraction.

The corporation is not an eternal structure, like a choir of angels. It is given to the creation of wealth under very material and temporal conditions; but it needs a discerning ethic to shape the legal constraints that govern its behaviors from the outside as well as a reconstructed ethic to help guide its internal life. Indeed, since Protestant thought nurtured the growth of the corporation in the first place, there are already strong echoes of theological history in notions of stewardship, work ethic, honest weights and measures, cooperation, trusteeship, quality products and services, fair prices and wages, development of workers' gifts, and professional duty. There is no obvious reason why these cannot again be recast for new global corporations.

Media

The sense of what ought to be done about the economy, particularly as it influences the infrastructures of social life in neighborhoods and families, as well as our relationships to neighbors beyond political borders through the corporations, is inevitably influenced by the media, which extends post-religious perspectives on the world further into cultural dominance. Religion, which is at its best related to but not identical with culture, may remain the chief bearer of ethical values; but it does so in a uncomprehending and often hostile environment, especially as portrayed by the media—which probably means that a hostility is latent in at least part of population, since the media provides what it perceives the people to want.

Although the deep influences of religion continue to shape our consciousness and the deep trajectories of our society in regard to economic matters, they do so in ways we no longer recognize and are not acknowledged among those institutions that shape popular consciousness. And without an awareness of the roots of or reasons for these structures or attitudes, they seem implausible or entirely due to malice. Those who are not familiar with the reasons why one would engage in material life for higher purposes often presume that lower purposes are the only compelling ones. Yet, basic views of wealth or poverty as blessing or curse, as deserved or unmerited, as something to be resisted as temptation, or accepted as pre-ordained lot or embraced as gift, have been deeply shaped by religion. And the place of charity, benevolence, diligence, thriftiness, festival, celebration, merit, fortune, and equality as marks of fidelity or virtue is distinctively stamped by religion in every world culture.

Even if Protestant orientations on these questions pervade our culture still, few know how or why. They are blotted out of public image and common discourse. And few Protestant leaders clearly articulate the grounds for these structures and attitudes when they do get access to the media. Some, indeed, are so overwhelmed by the complexities of the debates that they simply echo the non- or anti-religious theories they hear.

The Protestantism and Capitalism Debate

To be sure, some of these debates are rather intense and not entirely settled. Perhaps the most paradigmatic post-Marxist debate is about the "Protestant ethic" with its "this-worldly asceticism" as the basic driving force of modernization, what Max Weber treated as the "spirit of capitalism." Weber's thesis has been disputed for most of the century, with a number of fascinating twists.

Karl Marx had claimed (and Werner Sombart later argued) that the Jews created capitalism as a part of their general propensity to haggle for a better deal. But Weber repudiated this anti-Semitic suggestion and its presumption that economic interests generate great religions. After Weber, the Italian economist A. Fanfani argued that, indeed, Protestantism had produced capitalism, and that, thank God, Catholics would never do such a thing. Joining the debate, Ernst Troeltsch, the German historian of Christian social ethics, argued that certain kinds of Protestantism gave unintended impetus to modernization, including the rationalization of the economy; and the Hegelian laborite R. H. Tawney, suggesting that he, too, was supplementing Weber, turned the argument around to claim that capitalism augmented Protestantism in that it became the faith of choice for those who wanted to get rich and break the constraints of decent Christian behavior.

Later, Kurt Samuelsson doubted any relationship between religion and economic development at all, but the leading social theorist of the post World War II period, Talcott Parsons, rebutted his doubt with the argument that Protestantism denied the utility of priestly mediation and thereby called modern humanity from patriarchal dependency to individual initiative and pluralistic institutions. More recently, Rubem Alves claimed that just these features of export Protestantism gave rise, in Third World countries, to enclaves of alienated and repressed individuals who could not freely participate in the indigenous cultural fiestas of life; while the British social psychologist Robert Furnham argued that this individualization and compulsive work-orientation is what is wrong with people today at the top.

Today, Michael Novak, a Roman Catholic neo-liberal, argues that Catholicism, having finally purged its traditional anti-modernism and overcome its socialist sympathies thanks to a Polish pope, is now better positioned than faltering Protestantism to guide a morally revitalized capitalism into the next century. And David Martin, perhaps the leading scholar of new religious development in South America, argues that Pentecostal and Evangelical movements are again generating a new asceticism, complete with a demand for stable families, responsible communities, and economic development among the poor in Latin America and in similar communities of Africa and Asia.

This debate could occupy a complete college course and can

teach us much about the interaction of religious ethics and economic forces both in real social history and in the minds of the interpreters of social history. It also reveals the unsettled character of the debate of what one means in the post-Marxist period by "religious ethic" and "capitalist economy." But the whole debate hinges in part on the question of why people do what they do, why we do what we do. Is modern humanity, are we ourselves, driven by convictions or so socialized into the preprogrammed cultural values produced by the convictions of our forebears that we have come to love the "iron cage" of compulsive production? Or are we driven by our obsessive and insatiable wants that press us to work ever more efficiently so that we can consume more and more in a mad devouring of the world? The problem is, it may be both.

One side of Protestant-influenced culture accents the ascetic, disciplined, rational attitude toward life that was the most important force in establishing modern patterns of production. The other side of Protestant-influenced culture is the self-indulgent, romantic one that derives from the impulse to discern one's own inner state and needs as the clue to authentic living. It desires what the first makes; it consumes what the first produces. It attunes its inner impulses to discerning needs and seeks above all to express its felt wants, the spontaneous satisfaction of which is held to be the clue to authentic being. Our lives are morally split. Some understand not only capitalism but modernity, globalization, and modern life generally as the restrained and careful stewardship of time, energy, resources, and talent to improve the soul, aid the common life, and build a better world. Others see capitalism, and everything shaped by its impact, as given to self-will, unfettered consumerism, and a quest for the egocentric satiation of passing moods and fugitive feelings while demanding that economics pillage the world for the privileged.

Reference to these several views ignores a number of studies that argue that Islam (as in Indonesia, after breaking with the Arabic culture) or Confucianism (as in the Asia rim countries, once middle kingdom imperialism and its literati domination is broken) or Buddhism (as in Japan, after joining with Shinto and Confucianism to bring revisions in the Tokugawa period) can also generate Protestant-like ascetic drives and consumerist lusts. Nor does it treat the growing practice in Indian corporations to have management training sessions drawn from the *Bhagadva Gita*.

Oddly, no one would seriously treat the world cultures today

35

without reference to the basic religious influences that have defined the peculiar shapes of those cultures, those societies, and their economies. Can anyone seriously treat the economic life of India without reference to the social ethics of Hinduism, or of Egypt without speaking of the ethics of Islam, or of the Asian rim without mentioning Buddhism or the Confucian heritage? Yet many try to speak of the driving forces that have shaped modernization in the West and the new pressures toward globalization without reference to any religious ethic. Unless Christian leaders take up the question again, they will not be able to understand the profound religious impulses that are intertwined with economic life as it is, and forfeit all opportunity to reconstruct it in the future.

The Reconfiguration of Civil Society

Today, it seems to many pastors that the relationship of Christian ethics to the fabric of civil society and economic life—the moral and spiritual infrastructure of family life and community, the trustworthiness of corporate and commercial life, the images by which our view of personal and social identity is formed—is eroding. They may be too pessimistic, but we would be foolish not to take such a perception with great seriousness.

In regard to family life, for instance, pastors continue to perform weddings and baptisms and confirmations, and to encourage young people to prepare themselves to do something useful in the world. But they also find themselves dealing with both the sad loneliness of lovelessness and with bitter debates about unwed mothers, irresponsible fathers, divorces, dysfunctional relationships, damaged children, and violence in the home. They face issues of child abuse and wife-beating and date rape. It is not at all clear that people with whom they minister know how to love.

Nor is it obviously better on the international scene, in spite of the promising character of a number of developments. Images of terrified and starving refugees haunt the news, and compassion cools with resignation and disgust at the seeming incapacity of the world community to do much more than wring its hands and avert its eyes from Bosnia in Europe, Burma in Asia, Rwanda in Africa, and El Salvador in South America.

We have seen terrors enough in this past century; but we face a new problem. The horrors of the twentieth century were rooted in attempts to create more "liberty," "solidarity," or "equality" according to some more or less plausible theory. Some of these ideologies we now know to have been demonic, but they at least tried to supply some rationale or justification, usually based on some theory of nature or history or humanity. Protestantism, wherever its commitment to freedom was vigorous (but more wherever it had a profound and vertebrate understanding of holiness) resisted the distortions of family life and sexuality, the exploitations by economic elites of workers and the public, and the systematic polluting of consciousness through manipulation of the media, wherever these brought violations of the laws, purposes, and mercies of God.

What is remarkable about the lack of civility at both the local and the international level today is that it does not even bother to pretend a justification. We have no visible satans, and efforts to conjure them up seem contrived. We have only the black holes of spiritlessness, amorality, and intellectual blankness. The devil has taken a new form. Today's evil has no grand design, certainly not one that attempts to shape the institutions, laws, morality, or religion that offers meaning beyond the mere this-sidedness of life. Ideas of, or quests for, a vision of holiness meet only blank stares where they do not evoke the hostile conviction that having a firm point of view, a theory or a philosophy or a religion, is the cause of evil in the world.

Some of this may be due to an understandable rage at the way modern society has treated some people, especially unskilled and minority labor; and many are afraid, after colonialism, of anything that even appears to be "imposed" value. Yet the problem is deeper. We are unable to form policies to deal with this rage—or its causes—because we do not have a basis for our personal behaviors. Nor do we have public policies when our public is greater than the nation state, nor can we sustain a global vision if we have persons unable to see standards beyond their interests.

The subordination of the notion of the laws and purposes and callings of God to the notion of freedom has produced a new antinomian way of viewing the world; nearly a generation of Protestants have tried to reconstruct Christian theology on one version of this worldview, under the general title "liberation." The passion for justice in this movement remains as a monument of faithfulness; but only after the fall of the Berlin Wall and the collapse of liberation movements in most parts of Asia, Africa, and Latin America did Christians begin to question the hidden assumptions of this view, both in terms of the self-sufficiency of liberty as a goal and in terms of its analysis of the causes of oppression. The allies of Protestantism, in historic struggles for freedom—the Enlightenment, Romanticism, liberalism, and Marxism—proved incapable of reconstructing civil society.

Many heirs of the Reformation who adopted liberationist thought have sacrificed much for what they thought would set at liberty those who are oppressed. But the glasses through which they read the world betrayed them. They saw threats on the right rather clearly; they remain blind in the left eye. In spite of the overwhelming evidence, they failed to discern, report, and criticize the horrors wrought by the ideas they embrace. Although few are, in any dogmatic sense, Marxists or Communists, socialist categories of thought have cut the channels of mind by which many of the most sensitive minds of our day think about social issues. While, for instance, many insist that we gain a nuanced idea of the varieties of socialism, enormous numbers of Protestant leaders allow unqualified socialist definitions of capitalism to govern their thought. Yet, when they are taken as guides to social ethics and public policy, they reinforce nationalistic mercantilism, they compound poverty, they make inequalities between peoples worse, and they make the reconstruction of civil society more difficult.

It is completely justifiable, therefore, that otherwise faithful church members feel righteous anger about the ways in which some liberationist church leaders have manipulated the gospel, the instrumentalities of the church, and their religious authority to raise consciousness in directions that ultimately dehumanize and lead to social breakdown. While it is true that some of the hostility to liberationism is due to resistance among people who want to protect their own interests, it is also the case that many thoughtful believers simply do not believe that the liberationist account of social and economic life is true, its ethic just, its program viable.

It is neither possible nor desirable for Protestantism to return to some golden age of the past, in part because it would be difficult to know when to go back to, and in part because we must now face a new future. Nor can or should Protestantism seek to retrieve the theocratic hegemony that it sought at times in Europe or the messianic pretenses to establish a "Christian nation" that some parts of our heritage attempted in America. But Protestantism must reclaim its constructive and capacious willingness to engage complex civilization at all its levels as it forms a fresh Public Theology for an age that faces disarray.

Neo-Liberalism and Neo-Conservatism

Each sector of civil society, including family, corporation, and media, bears within it values that guide human behavior in the economy. Insofar as these give interpretive meaning to work and celebration, to individuality and community, to expectation of change or acceptance of station, economic life and work are guided by meanings and relationships that are not, in any narrow sense, economic or confined to "the private sector" at all. They are actually social and public. Even if Protestantism must leave its recent alliance with liberation behind, it must continue to hold a suspicion of those reductionist, often rationalistic economic theories that travel under the name of "neo-liberalism" and understand humans only as *homo economicus*.

There is little doubt but that people attempt to calculate rationally various advantages, costs, and benefits, and try to improve the quality of their lives; but what counts as advantage, as cost, or benefit, or improvement, or quality is profoundly stamped by the relational and moral fabric of human sociality, and even more by the deep legacies of religious tradition. It does not help us to understand economic life if we rule these factors out of the discussion and claim that all issues boil down to a rational choice by individuals to gain more and lose less. Such calculations, in fact, distort the soul, as those alert to qualitative issues know when they see the shallow and callous character of what many take to be advantage, benefit, or quality. That is why, one suspects, clergy and theologians find economics, as it is so often presented, so uninteresting, distorting, and ideological. Even when it is trying to be scientific, it blocks out the most important features of economic life and thus emerges as a reductionistic abstraction in the employ of interests other than what is life-giving and life-serving.

Insofar as "neo-liberalism" depends on this view of economic life and fails to frame it in a larger social and ethical vision, Protestantism must oppose it as much as it does liberationism. In fact, a key reason that so many turned to liberation thought is that it often offered the only current, vocal critique of these reductions available to non-specialists. Even if the technical achievements of economics must be honored, and many who oppose it grudgingly do so, it turns out that "neo-liberal" economists, who dominate the mainstream, in fact live their lives on the basis of values and commitments that do not find a place in their theory.

"Neo-conservatives" know that. They are often the political allies of neo-liberals in opposing the agenda of liberationism; but they know that neither neo-liberalism nor neo-conservatism can stand as an ideology in its own right. It is more than a grammatical point to note that the terms "neo-liberal" and "neo-conservative," like "Protestant," are adjectives, not nouns; they depend on something substantive beyond themselves to gain potency. Thus, there may be neo-conservative Christians or neo-liberal Jews, neo-conservative Muslims or neo-liberal Hindus, or, for that matter, neo-conservative pagans or neo-liberal humanists. There are certainly neo-conservative Democrats and neo-liberal Republicans; but what defines the deeper trajectory of thought and behavior will, in each case, turn out to be a theology or social philosophy that constitutes the substance of their convictions. Neo-conservatives have to be assessed, then, on the basis of what it is that they are trying to conserve under new conditions.

Neo-conservative stances involve reaction against change, as seen from their substantive base-point, while neo-liberals are quite open to the deconstruction of the past. Liberation thought, of course, assumes that social change will bring more freedom and solidarity. Against that presumption, neo-conservatism sees in the social changes embraced by liberation movements a rejection of traditional practices and classical wisdom that kept freedom (and, not incidently, some privileges) from succumbing to chaos. The problem with neo-conservatism is that it does not want to give an account of why the traditional practices and classical wisdom are the only things that can preserve the vital aspects of freedom without succumbing to anarchy. Traditional practice and wisdom may indeed be valuable, but tradition is dynamic and ongoing. It changes and develops. And wisdom has never been confined to one tradition or period of the past. To say that we must conserve something because it is ours, because we were formed by it and remain embedded in it, or because it defines our personal, social, or cultural identity is precisely to deny the possibility of growth, new insight, and above all conversion.

Protestants may well respect traditions, their own and other people's, but they are not and cannot be the defining center of loyalty. Indeed, traditions that protect unjust privilege or that block out the possibilities of conversion and transformation are viewed by Protestants as contrary to scripture, reason, and the redemptive experience of grace. The critique of liberation thought by Protestants, thus, dare not mean the automatic embrace of either one of these reactions against it. Temporary alliances may well be made, just as classical parts of the Protestant tradition have allied with Renaissance, Enlightenment, Romantic, and liberal developments to hold more dangerous trends at bay, and just as very significant parts of Protestantism supported anti-colonial movements with the liberationists.

On the whole, however, such alliances are strategic and temporary. The longer view recognizes that Protestantism seeks a better way of discerning and addressing social issues, of defending justice, engaging the future, and ordering the common life. It does not merely react against change, but seeks to discern the laws, purposes, and callings of God, as known through the common grace of creation, the providential grace of the history of the people of God and the special grace in Jesus Christ. These are what can guide the use of freedom into obedient, purposeful, and vocationally fitting channels. The substantial noun for "protestant" is Christian—viewed not as simply another tradition, but as a definitive relationship to God through Christ that renders an eagerness to participate in God's reshaping of the whole of life in holiness.

The Word and Social Forces

The heritage of the Reformation is in agreement with other branches of Christianity in regard to many of its quarrels with liberationism, neo-liberalism, and neo-conservatism. What determines the structure of civil society and the decisive patterns of culture is finally not the human will as it appears in revolutionary praxis, in rational choice regarding gain, or in privileged traditions. Nor is it some form of determinism that overrides freedom—the genetically given intelligence (i.e., the "bell curve"), the logic of evolution (i.e., "sociobiology"), the stage of technology (i.e., the "means of production"), the existence of private property (i.e., "control over the means of production"), the division of classes (i.e., "who has control over the means of production"), the interests of the dominant classes that generate a culture (a "ruling ideology") to

41

maintain control, nor even the establishment of militaries and police to enforce the ruling ideology (i.e., "the coercive state"). These material forces always play a role in social history; but they are not omnipotent or decisive in society even when they influence many decisions. They are secondary to the question of the basic structures of meaning and the principles of right and wrong, good and evil, truth and falsehood that exist in the consciousness of the people.

A central tenet of Protestantism bears on this question: Protestantism believes in the power of the Word. In its narrow sense, this refers to the creative self-disclosure of God in the accounts of creation, covenant, prophecy, and wisdom of the Holy Scriptures, especially as they point to the life, teachings, death, and resurrection of Jesus Christ. More broadly, this implies that what is preached, taught, studied, believed, and confessed is more powerful than its contexts—historical or contemporary. The Word transcends the context and names, and thereby unveils the latent meanings in the material contexts of life, precisely as it identifies and invokes the more ultimate and powerful guiding power that actually determines human, intellectual, social, and economic existence. Therefore Protestants alert to the implicit meanings of their own tradition resist seeing theology as derivative, or dependent, or as merely a part of culture, especially when culture is held to be secondary to what is most real. This is where we differ from many liberationists, neo-liberals, and neo-conservatives.

This theological point is, simultaneously, an ethical and sociohistorical point. Over time, the way people order their life together under the impress of their deepest convictions determines more surely than any other force or set of forces the fabric of civilization. More than anything else, the socially embodied conviction is what orders life and includes or excludes any gene-pool population as full members of the human community; it is what legitimates or delegitimates altruistic as opposed to aggressive sociobiological drives; it is what enhances or inhibits the use of technology to intervene in nature; it is what forms or deforms the sense of justice with regard to the laws of property; it is what expands or constricts the interactions of classes in society; and it is what gives authority to, or denies the authority of, the polities of state and its coercive policies.

At their core, societies like individuals are irreducibly religious, and social analysis is false if it does not focus centrally on this fact. It is no wonder that thousands of pastors become quickly bored with

42

social analysis that fails to deal with this dimension of life, and burn out trying to do everything with poor tools. The social realities they know firsthand are rooted in religious and theological issues; but the tools they are given to deal with these realities lack all reference to what is most important—the religious and theological perspectives they learn are inarticulate about their social implications.

Spirit forms matter more than matter forms spirit, although without material creation the creative power of spirit remains unrecognized. Conviction guides interests more than interest guides conviction, although without becoming incarnate in interests, shaping them, convictions float in the air of cant. Belief shapes culture more than culture shapes belief, although without embodiment in culture, belief remains idiosyncratic speculation. Since the heart of civil society is more surely religious than anything else, what is decisive, also, for economics is the kind and quality of religion that becomes incarnate in the ethos of civilization.[3]

The implications of this point are vast. When the Berlin Wall collapsed, more fell than simply a Marxist-Leninist approach to politics in a command economy, despite what those liberationists who wish to minimize the size of the earthquake might argue. What fell was also more than the triumph of neo-liberal, rational-choice economics, and more than neo-conservative traditions that protected privileged freedom. What fell was a post-religious, post-theological way of understanding civil society and economic realities. Secular prophecy—right, left, and backward—proved incapable of discerning the real forces of history.

We are, as many eagerly say about every other area of life, in the midst of a major paradigm shift; although the resistance to the shift in this area is substantial. Indeed, many who poured years of their lives into celebrating and working for Marxist liberation movements in Latin America or Africa or Asia or among North American minority communities feel betrayed by history, and tend to blame the failures on neo-liberalism or neo-conservatism, on "traditionalism" or, more simplistically, the "radical right." Similarly, those neo-liberals and neo-conservatives who chortle at new trends against "liberalism," but simply strip the poor of freedom and increase the freedom of the privileged, will soon find that history will betray them as well. The issue is not left and right, it is the power of the Word, with its freedom and order, in encounter with material forces and social interests. They will join; they should join; the Word will guide—slowly over time, faster if it is clear. What Word will it be? On what shall it be based?

What Else Fell?

The problem is all the more difficult because what fell was a series of other conceptual maps by which many contemporary thinkers have organized their views of social and economic life. One of the decisive ones is the resistance to all forms of duality—a resistance that leads to a flat, this-worldly monism. We can see resistance toward that monism in all the great religious traditions. Roman Catholic, Evangelical, and Orthodox traditions have begun to reassert a Christian dualism, which asserts a reality beyond this world, beyond positivism. Parallel accents are also obvious in much of resurgent Islam and in Hindu Nationalism (*Hindutva*),[4] in spite of the fact that Islam's radical monotheism is sometimes inclined to a spiritual monism (as in the Sufi tradition), and monism is implicit in several of the "orthodox" views of traditional Hindu philosophy. Nevertheless, these traditions feel compelled to join Christian efforts to resist secular-historicist ways of comprehending life and social history that make this life in this world the only frame of reference.

Protestants know that other forms of dualism can lead to great difficulty. Dualisms that correlate stereotyped views of male and female, white and black, rich and poor, or noble and base, lead to all sorts of arrogance and have been used to justify a variety of dominations for which there is no theological or ethical justification whatsoever. But since all these differences are present in human experience, humanity needs something beyond human historical and social experience that puts them into a relative rather than in absolute perspective.

The significance of this more ultimate dualism lies in its implicit challenge to the view that we can best understand and guide civil society by attending *only* to the changing dynamics of power relations, and that, therefore, neither an appeal to God nor a relationship to God is necessary to the analysis of culture and civilization. Insofar as Protestant ethics has itself tended to engage in social analysis and social theory without reference to religion, morality, or theology, and then, only later, to ask the question of how theology and ethics ought to respond, it has embraced a primary monism on the one hand and a secondary dualism on the other. But that exactly reverses the classic

Protestant priority. This classic view sees a basic dualism that is resolved only provisionally in history, society, and identity. Even the ultimate end of historical, social, and personal life is said to be pluralistic and complex—it is a "city," not a cosmic egg.

Central to Protestantism, and to other forms of Christianity as well, is the worship of God. God is not the world, and cannot be reduced to the world or to anything in the world, whether icon or idol, sacrament or principality, consciousness or creativity, religious conviction or creed. This sense of the otherness of God is shared with Judaism and Islam and some forms of Hinduism as well. To be sure, the doctrine of the Trinity partly separates us from these traditions, for it speaks of the pluralistic and relational nature of God and of how this God, being other than this world as its Creator, is also through Jesus Christ and by the power of the Holy Spirit present to the world. However, the insistence on the basic dualism of God and the world (within which all Christian doctrines of "two-nature Christology" and "spiritual body," etc., make sense) is properly held to be central to the faith and to the accurate grasp of reality.

Protestants hold that we can know enough about the triune God to grasp the truth of this holiness that is other than the way things are in the world. In fact, this truth is the clue to all other truth; the idea that humanity could get along without this reality—that persons could be formed, enduring relationships constructed, and civilization sustained without reference to this reality—is simply false. To be sure, persons are formed, relationships are made, and societies come into existence, for a time, without overt and conscious knowledge of or reference to God. However, they are simply coasting. They live off the spiritual capital and moral treasury built into the fabric of life by generations, now long deceased, that were very concerned about God. The monists leach the core out of life and cannot replenish it.

Current anti-dualist arguments often, and oddly, also divide the world into an artificial dualism of determinate, concrete experience and dependent, abstract conception. This map has hidden in it a presumption about the logical, historical, and moral priority of concrete base and substructure over abstract conception and superstructure. It remains, however, a monism because there was no real "otherness" to the second, abstract, side. The superstructure is seen as a function of the substructure that interacted, after its functional generation, so as to modify the substructure. It is like a mirror with short-term memory, one that retains past reflections for a while and by that retention modulates new reflections. But this is not a dualism in any theological sense; it is only a dialectic within interacting parts of a singular, non-transcending reality.

All the World Is Divided into Three Parts

Gradually, still another conceptual map was developed that has deeply shaped our perceptions, even if it stands in awkward relationship to those mentioned before. By the 1960s, nearly everyone began to speak of the First, Second, and Third Worlds. These terms had been introduced by President Sukarno of Indonesia at the meeting of the Non-Aligned Nations in Bandung in 1955. These ideas correlated with some Western neo-liberal theorists who spoke in terms of nations as "developed," "developing," and "underdeveloped" and they were adopted in the next decade by Willy Brandt's democratic-socialist program, "Toward a New International Economic Order," which was later voted by the United Nations General Assembly as a "united determination" in UN Resolutions 3201 and 3202.[5]

These terms became the analysis of choice for those all around the world who opposed "the Western Capitalist" model of development as well as "the Eastern Communist" one, and who wanted to give priority to the economically weaker regions of the world. These ideas were adopted by leaders of the World Council of Churches in its resolutions in the 1970s and by the Roman Catholic bishops of Latin America in the 1980s. They remain as part of the common vocabulary and profound moral loyalties among Christians. To be "for" the "Third World" and to stand prophetically "against" the evils of the "First" and the "Second" became unofficial dogma, even where various parties tilted toward the First or the Second in primal loyalties. To challenge the basic conceptual map has, until quite recently, been to risk unofficial excommunication.

To put the notion of "world" in the plural is itself a very imaginative move. It also had great consequences in a world that had just completed the second of two world wars and constituted a United Nations on the basis of documents which spoke of "one world" and "universal human rights." The notion of a world meant something complete in itself; something whole and somehow inviolable. One could think of things beyond the world, but they were of a quite

46

different order, and this typology showed no interest in anything transcendent.

What irony! The earth was though of as a whole, but promptly divided by new criteria, with the implication that each "world" is its own totality, its own political and economic arrangements, its own social fabric, its own cultural vision of meaning, its own religious integrity, and its own ethical matrix of values. These guaranteed that each world was justified in treating its people the way it saw fit. What could not be done was to claim that some ethical principle or insight of faith was true for all. The worst thing that could be done, within this new dogma, would be to impose something from one world on another one, as if cultures and societies and religions or economies or political orders had ever, in the entire history of humanity, fit the anthropologists' dream of a globe full of whole and complete citadels of life and meaning:

The "First World" (primarily Western Europe and North America) was taken to be individualistic, post-religious, democratic, capitalistic, technologically advanced, and rich, with a small, poor under class.

The "Second World" (Eastern Europe and some client states abroad) was taken to be collectivist, anti-religious, totalitarian, socialistic, technologically advancing, and committed to an economic equality that was not yet realized.

The "Third World" (most of Asia, Africa, and Latin America) was taken to be communitarian, religious, necessarily authoritarian in view of weak institutions and the relatively low percentage of people equipped to exercise modernizing leadership, properly nationalistic after colonialism, technologically underdeveloped, and poor— although with a small, reactionary, rich upper class who, supported by North Atlantic multinational corporations, kept the masses poor and destroyed the ecosphere at will.

A great number of religious and moral advocates of a wider international consciousness rallied around this idea of the "Third World." They connected it to ideas and movements for the reduction of nuclear weapons, and to the "dependency theory" in economics, which attributed poverty in the "Third World" to exploitations by the "First World" and proposed to overcome it by populist movements at the local level and socialist policies at the national level, both supported by the "Second World." This view also criticized various "development theories" that were encouraged by the World Bank or the International Monetary Fund.

47

This set of convenient fictions meant that it was fairly easy to offer an analysis of any situation without having to fuss with all the data about social or theological history. One simply consulted one's social location and inferred appropriate states of consciousness, relationship, and conviction—until, of course, the proletariat of Poland organized Solidarity with the help of the Roman Catholic Church against the Communists; the populist pro-democratic demonstrations of East Germany developed in and around the Lutheran churches to alter socialism; the Evangelical Protestants joined with the liberal democrats of Nicaragua to overthrow the Sandanistas; the "liberated" former colonies of Africa and Asia began to privatize, deregulate, and seek investment from multinational corporations; and the masses of the Soviet Union, with enormous ambiguity and uncertainty, turned toward something resembling constitutional democracy and free-market capitalism, supported by Orthodox Christianity.

Some try to save the theory by simplifying the geography: "the West" and "the Rest," or "North"/"South," but these so oversimplify the world that they are soon recognized as only caricatures. The West is now present everywhere, and the rest refuse to stay at home. No place is immune from globalization and multiculturalism, and every place has its stratifications of opportunity, wealth, and privilege. Others shift from geography to numbers, speaking of the "Two-Thirds World" as the poorer peoples of the world in contrast to the "One-Third" who have relative security or even wealth. Both these moves seek to keep the paradigm of a two-class conflict to understand our situation, and run directly into all the problems that earlier socialism faced.

However, increasing numbers of social problems internal to various societies refuse to sort themselves on this division. Is the defense of civil and political human rights against centralized state power in Indonesia and China to stand with the "Two-Thirds" or the "One-Third World"? How does one chart the resistance to increasing numbers of abortions around the world and the defense of "family values" at home by poor, rural Baptists and blue-collar, center-city, unionized Catholics and suburban, Republican Anglicans? Does the transfer of capital and technology, the building of factories, and the employment of landless workers in Central America and Southeast Asia by First World business leaders responsive to the requests of post-colonialist governments enhance or inhibit "Third World" values?

Not only does the typology fail to congeal the multiple variables it pretends to include, it does not address the debates it purports to handle, in spite of the fact that the current habits of thought jam the issues into dysfunctional maps. They are really believed today only by the theologically impaired.

Perhaps We Should All Turn "Green"

If socialism has failed and liberationism is confused, if neo-liberal and neo-conservative agendas are dependent on more than they can supply, if Sukarno's guide to the world no longer edifies, and if the left-right spectrum embedded in these conceptual maps does not grasp the realities behind contemporary economic life—if all of these betray or distort theology—should we then turn to the ecological theory that has come to prominence among process theologians and eco-feminists? This is now the thought world to which many critics of modernity turn.[6]

This is a doubtful solution. The reason is that these points of view tend to be anti-technological. Ecological theory as adopted by Christian thinkers is seldom anti-scientific, but it is deeply suspicious of technology. Christians who subscribe to ecological theory often see technology as destructive of nature and disruptive of community. And, since God is often understood in terms of naturalistic and communitarian terms, technology is rendered anti-theological. The opposite, however, is more likely the case. Technology may preserve creation, build new possibilities of community, and be both true to and dependent upon theology. Such historical and systematic points entail several assumptions about our condition:

(1) We have some freedom about how life is to be lived; the decisive ethical question is how we ought to use that freedom and what should guide it.

(2) Humans have only a limited "natural" way of knowing how things ought to be changed. We cannot rely on nature to guide us fully in this area, for nature is what is changed by technology.

(3) Technology involves both a freedom to change things and the necessity of reordering them. We are not bound by the way things are; we can change things, but for things to work they must fit an order distinct from the way we find them.

(4) Those cultures influenced by a theological ethic are able to generate and sustain a technology that does not destroy more than

it reconstructs, for theology provides the most life-giving vision of a normative order beyond the natural one.

(5) It is possible to discuss such matters in public discourse and not only in the internal life of faith communities.

It certainly looks as if technology will shape our future. The emerging global economy, the new communications networks, and the developing modes of learning and healing and cooking are all technological. But technology only comes into being when an ethos is guided by a metaphysical-moral vision beyond technology itself, a vision that tells us that we can and should figure out how things work in order to alter the way they work. The fact that we think things can and should work better in an altered way is one of the deepest permanent legacies of a theological point of view on modernity. Without that, humanity has an ontological propensity to settle into the way things are, as can be seen in a number of failed experiments in technological transfer without value transfer.

The modern ecological movement is, in concert with this ontological propensity, rooted in the view that we ought to live according to the natural logic of how things work, although different wings of the movement differ on whether the natural logic of things is best understood in terms of a natural organic system (Gaia), or according to an evolutionary-historical dynamic (Process). Both are rooted in the doctrine that a primal guidance system built into the nature of things is the logic that ought to be followed, and both accent a model of reality that involves a dynamic totality of interactive sub-systems that modernity is destroying by its technological domination.

These views are closer to those traditions that derive from the Reformation than liberationist, neo-liberal, or neo-conservative ideologies, for while they recognize a degree of freedom in human life, they recognize that this freedom must be ordered and guided in accord with some ultimate understanding of reality. Yet an ambiguity remains as to how to assess these problematic allies in our midst.

There is little doubt about it: ecological/environmental awareness is one of the several great entrées into cross-cultural thinking today. Along with human rights and the emergence of a pervasive matrix of global economic interdependence, the issue of the future of the biophysical planet in relationship to the future of civilization poses a basic theological-ethical question: Are there common problems that demand concerted human attention beyond the particularities of culture, class, ethnicity, nationality, and gender? How we sort out this issue will have major implications for both human rights and economics. These perspectives raise the question of whether there are (and whether modern humanity can reliably know if there are) general norms and principles that do, or should, or could guide the common life. The problem, however, is that they tell us that ecological issues should have a *prima facie* priority over other forms of universal thinking, such as human rights or theological ethics, for it is to "nature" that they appeal when they want to show that some aspect of life is "really real" or truly valid. Indeed, if it turns out that if this or that philosophy (or theology) evokes, promotes, or reinforces a human tendency to violate what is natural, many suspect that the matter is settled. To call something "natural" is, for many today, to enter the court of final appeal.

Because of this ontological propensity, many see the source of the ills of modern technology, and hence of modern economics, in the mistaken, dualist notion that God is other than the world, and that in our obedience to God we may be called upon to change the world. That creates a further dualism of nature and history that obscures the embeddedness of all things historical in nature, and the natural tendency for things to change, on their own, over time. Here again we find a powerful anti-dualism, but one that leads to a vision of restraint and discipline, not liberation.

The argument is, in outline, simple: nature and history and divinity are bound together in one seamless web; they are under threat; they must be saved; we must save them; and we can do so by altering how we think about the world. Ironically, many of those who want to protect nature are in fact quite idealistic. They believe that ideas make a difference and are not simply the by-product of social location. Thus, failures in economic, social, and ecological life are due to failures of a philosophical, ethical, and theological sort. Especially culpable here are abstract modes of thought that separate history from nature, self from society, theory from practice, or God from the world. But it is a serious question as to whether we ought to accept this anti-dualism, and the reasons are both theological and sociological.

On Nature and Creation

Many are confused theologically about the nature of nature. It is not necessary to reject everything that comes from the Enlightenment to point out that it conflated the terms creation and nature.

Since then, when we speak of nature, we ordinarily mean the bio-physical universe, with the implicit understanding that its patterns and dynamics are the ultimate frame of reference: the way God wants things to be. In the attempt to avoid a transcendence that becomes dualistic, many are tempted to a naturalistic, geocentric, or evolutionary monism that loses theological and thus also human amplitude.

In contrast, when one speaks of creation, one signals that the biophysical universe is not the whole or the norm, but a temporal reality that is subject to norms and ends beyond it. Indeed, the notion of "fallen nature" reinforces the distinction. It suggests that, while traces of God's law and purposes are inevitably scripted into the deep character of all that is, the natural things of the world are out of order or confused of direction in one or another respect. It is not that finitude is *by itself* evil; but rather that finite reality has betrayed its original design, goal, and function.

To gear ourselves only into nature, thus, is to degenerate further. It is only by the knowledge of something other than nature that we know that the *status quo*, including the peril of ecological damage, is not as it should be. And it is only by grasping what is beyond nature that we resist either reverting to the *status quo ante* of organicism or plunging into the *fluxus quo* of process. Nature, including human nature, can only be rightly ordered and fulfilled by being trans-formed through a conversion—a sanctification, marked by crucifix-ion and resurrection—that brings a new quality of existence, one dominated by an humble righteousness, a renewed willingness to pursue God's purposes, and a drive to reconstruct the necessary institutions of the common life wherein people may find their call-ings in the midst of social change.

This basic theological insight has been obscured by certain classic distinctions between "natural law" and "revealed law" according to Reformed understandings, and rejected by a number of current developments in theology. But the costs may be extremely high, for the implications of this basic Reformation view may well be true not only of personal, moral, and spiritual life, or particular social arrange-ments, but of the entire biophysical cosmos as well. Certainly, the scriptural tradition states this in revealing images. There is no return to the simpler garden. The path backward to innocence is blocked by unassailable powers of destruction. And we are not to be led astray when we hear of wars or earthquakes or famines or tribulations of many kinds, and try to save ourselves by honoring that which is only temporal. Instead, the future points toward the universal, eternal city open to all peoples, to which and for which the creatures, plants, and natural resources are to be redesigned. Nature, in other words, has to be transformed to become what God intends it to be, to accord with standards that are not complete in nature itself. The faithful are to be witnesses to and agents of this transformation, and technology is one of the means to be used.

Contemporary naturalist theologies do seek to overcome some tensions between culture and nature, and some do strive to see both theologically. But these theologies tend to press culture toward nature and identify nature's "becoming" with the divine. It simply is not clear how this "immanentalization" of God could prove to be capable of facing the central ethical demand of our time—to use the technology that is now on the horizon to transform nature, simultaneously supporting the fabric of personal and interpersonal life and enhancing the global structures of a graceful, cosmopolitan civilization able to serve the whole of humanity. This would demand a loving, just, and stewardly dominion of nature, for the sake of humanity and in service of God. It is doubtful that the tendency to a monistic naturalism, implicit in much ecofeminist thinking and process thought or in the "Green" politics generally, can prompt us to accept this vocation or to discern how that ought to be done.

This theological point would, to be heard in our world, have to defend itself against the charge that it is the source of all our ills. But that case becomes easier to make on simply empirical grounds as data about the ecologically devastating conditions both in traditional, pre-technological societies and in the anti-theological, socialist societies of the former Eastern European countries become available. The accusation that theism generally, and Christianity particularly, and the Protestant ethic most especially, is the primary source of our environmental ills is an argument of escalating rhetorical intensity but of declining credibility.

The damage wreaked by the most anti-religious regimes of Eastern Europe, the non-Christian regions of the world, and the anti-Protestant traditions in, say, Latin America, is tremendous. Indeed, the World Health Organization found recently, as reported widely in the press, that "nowhere in the history of humanity have the air, the land, the water, and the people been more systematically poisoned" than in Eastern Europe. And the deepest ecological/economic crisis areas of Africa and Asia can hardly be said to be those areas most influenced by a commitment to a transcendent God in the Christian tradition. It appears to be the case, in fact, that monism, either naturalist or historicist, is what most dramatically degrades both the biosphere and humanity.

Besides, other issues are at stake. For many years it was held that what divided the humans from the beasts was the fact that, at a certain point in evolution, humans stood up and began to make tools, a development that allowed those with the larger brain capacity to adapt to the environment more quickly than others. But this argument does not account for the tool-making among some animals, or the fact that it is not only tool-using that allowed humans to cut more deeply into the surrounding world. It is more likely that the Reformed theological tradition has it right: humans were distinguished from the beasts when they knelt down and saw *themselves* as tools of a loving and just God, called to be stewards of the earth where it manifested God's designs and to redesign the world where it was fallen.

An Alternative Reading

The problem is this: Much of modern Protestantism has adopted socialist, liberationist, "Third World," left/right, or "Green" analyses of our present world situation, often combining them in various ways, and allowed the central social and ethical themes of Protestant theology to wither. Most people in the pews, much of the younger generation, and a great number of pastors and scholars who have patiently listened to these views for more than a decade, do not believe them. These adopted analyses are proving to be inadequate for the regeneration of the church, the reconstruction of a viable civil society in our cities and towns, and the construction of an ethic for today's global realities.

We are now forced to face phenomena that these maps obscured: the reality of a new global humanity, locked together in a confused welter of stratified parts that do not have a governing vision but do constitute a single, complex system. A great number of people feel they are being swept into a new and vast global pyramid that they did not create, that they do not understand, and that they do not know how to enter or resist. Further, many now feel that they are relegated to permanent uselessness at the bottom of the heap, or are on a slippery slide toward a lower place. At the same time, the familial, local, community, and even national political supports that they had previously relied on in times of trouble appear to be eroding before their very eyes. These widespread feelings reflect a realistic awareness that we live in a new historic period. The depth and range of this reality means that we have to review and revise our models of how things are and how they might be, for the adopted perspectives we have here examined only confuse the situation and clutter the ground that has to be cultivated.

We should take very seriously the sense of being on the bottom of a vast hierarchical pyramid. Hierarchy is ever the way the world is. It is the way most of it has always been. The ancient philosophies, east and west, which tried to grasp the basic structures of natural life, have all seen a profound and pervasive stratification that reaches from the heights to the depths, from the angels and spirits above to the dust and heat below, with every society populated with multiple levels of humanity in between. The ancients may have been correct when they incorporated it into their theological vision—more correct, in fact, than those who see hierarchy as the historical construction of elitists who may be overthrown by understanding the world in terms of two classes, liberating ourselves from domination, dividing up the world into sovereign regions, or returning to a "natural" organic community without hierarchy, a human harmony with nature beyond technological disruptions.

Certainly the Reformation traditions recognized in the common Christian heritage that a "great chain of being" was part of the deep structure of life: biblical, historical, contemporary and, inevitably, futuristic. There was no question whatsoever about the need for leadership, nor about the various ways in which people are differently gifted for various roles in life.

We should have a firmer grasp on the nature and character of hierarchy than we do. Many have tried to make the case that a dualism of God and the world brought about evil hierarchy. The case is doubtful on three counts.

First, hierarchy may not be an historical factor at all, but the very structure of nature—*fallen* nature, from a Protestant theological point of view. All ecological and evolutionary analysis appears to presume that the biological world is arranged in food-chains, and that the strong, the bright, the adaptive, and the prolific survive, whereas the weak, the dull, the settled, and the non-fertile die out. If this is the only source of our norms, life will remain brutal indeed.

55

Second, it is not altogether clear that every form of hierarchy is equally evil. Excellence suffers when every opinion and every capacity is viewed as necessarily equal to every other. This does not mean that we should not press for a situation in which every opinion can be registered and every capability respected. Yet no one seriously holds for very long the notion that the heads of the university, the government, the law courts, the pop charts, any large corporation, or the great cathedral churches of the world should be honored, get paid, or have the same daily duties as the newest janitor, the lowest soldier, the worst criminal, the shiest monotone, an untrained worker, or the most recently baptized baby—although we properly demand the protection of the dignity of each and try to see that they are not unduly disadvantaged by their position.

Third, the selective approval of hierarchy, where it recognizes genuine excellence, is necessary to the whole and supportive of all the members. In turn, the resistance to any hierarchy that oppresses unjustly seems to come into being precisely where a universal, transcendent God (and thus a transcendental vision of justice and equity) is taken as the central guide to personal and social life. It is on this basis that the oppressive and unjust "natural" hierarchies that appear everywhere are challenged, and efforts are made to redress the difficulties of those on the bottom as well as to restrain the aggressions of those on the top.

With the breakdown of civil society in our center cities, and the possibilities of a wider civil society appearing in the networks of global interaction that expand our horizons beyond the nation state, we are seeing the emergence of a new economic hierarchy. The question is how we ought to respond to it.

My central hypothesis is that in the faithful Protestant churches the ultimate questions are posed; thus the great dualism that can control and challenge hierarchy where it is evil, and preserve it where it supports life, is made vital in people's minds and hearts. They can then begin to encounter the world—equipped to accept hierarchy where it is in accord with God's intent, or recognized as part of the fall that is unalterable within the confines of history, and able to challenge hierarchy where it is contrary to God's intent. They are also enabled to transform the structure of things toward holiness where it is necessary and where we are called and empowered by God to do so. This means that we have to seek to learn of God's intent and see it as the clue to reading the way things are in the world.

A related hypothesis is that we can no longer expect that the modulation and selective critique or approval of hierarchy will come from increasing the power of the nation-state. It is now widely believed that we are at the end of the period begun with the Peace of Westphalia, the pact of 1648 that established the modern system of national sovereignty in law for Europe (with which Protestantism has lived for most of its history). This view of the common life is deeply entrenched in the consciousness of most of modernity. It promoted a system in which the nation-state established both a centralized mechanism to guide economies, and a national religion or ideology to legitimate its interests. When people think of an "us" or the "common good," that is what they mean.

The consequence of this development, embraced by many Protestants who turned to political action to guide all aspects of social well-being, has been quite ambiguous. On the one hand, the state became, for many, the means of overcoming traditional hierarchies that claimed special privilege. Never mind that it created in bureaucracy new forms of hierarchy; that was a small price to pay. Further, the state became the chief agent of modernization and the central moral and legal control system for the whole of society—including religion. Contemporary theological discussions become serious to many only when political and legal matters are up for debate at the national level; when moral and spiritual issues are debated in public, many read them only in terms of legal and political programs.

The chief alternative to the historic statism that has inclined modernity to fascism and communism in our century has been various forms of constitutional democracy. These offered limits to state authority, coupled with an independence of religion from the state and with the recognition that economics and politics work by distinct logics, both subject to the values of society. Political life and economic life, like education, medicine, and culture, are sub-sectors of civil society, where it is alive and vibrant; each is influenced by the whole in different ways. Further, the kind and quality of this influence depend upon the kind and quality of religion that is held by the people in the midst of the common life.

This is the most significant contribution of Protestant Christianity to social life, traceable from the Reformation through the Puritan drive to order freedom by the formation of covenanted association and of the disciplined will: it stands as a clear implication of the prophetic traditions and the formation of the church. Here is the drive to establish freedom *under law*, with the purpose of making the material and social fabric of historical life more holy, in accord with the diverse gifts and callings of people. It is this ordered freedom that bestowed on the world the right to organize, which eventuated in the relative independence of school and university, of political party, of publishing house and mass media, of hospitals and professional associations, of economic corporations and unions independent of state control—"voluntary associations" or "mediating structures." The primary task of the state, beyond providing for the common defense and maintaining law and order, is to establish conditions for these organizations to flourish.

These spiritual, social, and material forces, often working in concert, are the *real* public, the stuff of civil society. It is the vitality of these that determines the overall shape and well-being of the economy and the society. These are the structures that flesh out common understandings of what is right, what is good, and what is fitting to our situations, and thus what might count as justice. Indeed, we can see in the enormous and growing influence of such groups in the 1992 Rio Conference on Ecology, the 1993 Vienna Conference on Human Rights, and in the debates about the 1994 GATT agreements (the basis of the World Trade Organization). These, along with those who advocate or resist actions by the United Nations, the World Bank, the International Monetary Fund, and possibly the Law of the Sea (1996?), now impact every ethos and influence every matter of public policy in ways that previous maps of social reality simply did not grasp.

To reconstruct Protestant theological-social ethics, then, we must acknowledge the declining power of the state and the increasing power of non-governmental groups—including, above all, the religious institutions that are before our very eyes and beneath our very noses. We have falsely trained ourselves to attend to everything but those institutions that turn out to be the most politically, economically, and intellectually pertinent, precisely because they are the infrastructure of civil society. We wrongly tried to be as "relevant" as possible to a world we believed was becoming secularized.

If we can unclutter our minds from the various monisms that have tempted our generation, we may be able to seek out, recover, and recast the great theological themes that have led, in every culture influenced by them, to the generation and regeneration of this decisive level of civilizational formation. These themes are more likely than anything else to guide us in the future, and prevent our new global economic situation from becoming another fixed and sanctified hierarchical feudalism.[7] This will be, above all, the task of clergy and of theologically literate laity: they know how to build things from the inside out, not only from the bottom up or the top down.

Dealing with Hierarchy

It is likely, however, that pressures from beneath and from beyond the state will converge in a constellation of developments that will press toward a complex, stratified economic pyramid. For Protestants, it is both frightening to contemplate (and quite plausible to imagine) some 60 percent of the population of North America joining some 40 percent of the populations of Europe, 20 percent of the Asian Rim and Latin American countries, and 10 percent of Africa and the island cultures, to occupy the higher echelons of wealth, income, diet, health care, educational opportunity, and longevity. It does not stretch the imagination to foresee that some 10 percent of the American population will join perhaps some 60 percent of Africa, 40 percent of Asia and Latin America, and 20 percent of Europe to occupy the lower echelons of the world economy. Indeed, that is close to our present situation. Yet Protestants have a distinct constitutional immunity to too much hierarchy. It rubs against the ideal of the "priesthood of all believers." Perhaps that is why Protestant cultures tend to become middle class, even bourgeois; being too rich without charity for the poor—or remaining in poverty when opportunities exist to use God-given talents to overcome poverty—is profoundly sinful. If Protestantism is to help overcome the new world hierarchy—not merely shout against it, or try to withdraw into enclaves of piety or, worse, nationalistic protection—what economic theories can it adopt?

Three decades ago, Simon Kuznetz began to chart out the ways and conditions under which populations become common aggregates, form great pyramids, and gradually develop toward diamond-shaped patterns of income and wealth.[8] The great story of the last several centuries, he says, has been the formation of nations full of middle classes out of more local, more steeply pyramidal, economies. Periodically, when capitalization, technology, and social conditions allowed it, larger population groups formed, and these threw the pattern back toward a larger hierarchy; under certain conditions, however, new developments in the middle classes pressed the general contours of inevitably stratified society toward a rounder, fatter configuration.

For the moment, we leave to the side the fact that the most important story of this last century, in terms of economic development, is not the increased polarization of the classes, as both the "Old Left" of the 1930s and the "New Left" of the 1960s believed (and their heirs today still believe). The great story, when we keep the global picture in view, is the monumental growth of the middle classes. This has not always been the immediate experience of Americans, for much of this growth has been among previously impoverished peoples of the "Two-Thirds World" as they move into what are by American standards "lower middle classes." Further, that growth has sometimes occurred precisely as parts of the U.S. population has experienced the relative shrinking of opportunity. But in a globalizing economy we must be cautious about the projection of the American experience onto the world screen. American developments influence, but do not define or represent, the wider global situation.

On the whole, what we have seen is the complex interaction of three developments: (a) an increase of wealth among upper classes, which makes the economic pyramid taller, with both an increase of the distance between the top and the bottom and an increased number of gradations in between; (b) the horizontal extension of the base of the pyramid to include new population groups, especially internationally; and (c) a massive expansion of some, though not all, strata of the middle classes, reducing the percentage of those in abject poverty and increasing the number of those who have or who aspire to a "middle class" lifestyle.

These developments did not take place everywhere equally, and do not seem to be inevitable. In fact, Douglass C. North expanded the Kuznetz argument to show that the tendency to expand the middle and raise the status of large percentages of those on the bottom takes place most clearly where legal, social, and moral principles defend intellectual property, encourage education for all, facilitate trade through the construction of infrastructure, and demand honesty and fairness in trade. These encourage the formation of enterprises able to produce new wealth.[9]

Today we can see that those nations with expanding middle

classes are those which allow and encourage the formation of multiple corporations of a wide variety. One can most accurately predict the well-being of the people by calculating the number of corporations present per thousand of the population. Of course, behind the existence of corporations are all sorts of social supports and personal habits of mind that are deeply influenced by the fabric of civil society, in various forms and stages of formation or decomposition.

At present we are approximating a situation in which nearly all peoples are included in a vast global pyramid, peaked almost like an Eiffel Tower, much more inclusive than even the ancient societies of China, India, or the medieval West. We also seem to have a worldwide openness to the formation of corporations, although the weakest portions of the population seldom know how to form them. Corporations are already the chief operating unit of modern economic life, and those ill equipped to form, maintain, or even join them are likely be to permanently dependent; it is an open question as to whether corporations can serve those not already a stakeholder in them and whether they can become all they could be in terms of creating wealth for the common good. For now, it is enough to ask whether Protestantism can help form the civil society, including the corporations, on a wider scale that would support the formation of new middle classes everywhere, whether it should do so, and if so, how it can do so.

It is not difficult to presume that, unless the system is to freeze into a fixed caste system, those peoples who have access to certain kinds of social resources that will prepare them for life in a cosmopolitan world will be better able to cope. The evidence is rather clear as to what is needed. We can see it in certain immigrant populations, and we can see it in certain cultures: stable families, a high regard for schooling, disciplined acceptance of delayed gratification, a fascination with technology, a cultural identity that is open to interaction with people of many lands and traditions, and, above all, a sense of religious duty to change the self and change the world for purposes other than private gain. It is surely moral to live off the profits of a good business; but it is just as surely a moral disaster to live only for profits. The best corporations live for the creation of good products and services, that is, for the creation of wealth. What they do is measured by profits, and no one should trust an economic institution that does not manifest and measure them well over time. Yet profits are not the meaning of life. Those groups or societies that foster

61

wider, deeper attitudes are likely to enhance the chances that their populations will find an improving position in the global pyramid, and those who do not will find themselves left as charity cases.

In the long run, what will be decisive in all this is not, as previous generations believed, a class warfare, although it is difficult to imagine that some will not become preoccupied with position in a vast stratification. Those are aspects of complex civility that both classical India and China, not to mention ancient Egypt, the Middle Ages in the West, the pre-Columbian societies of South America, and the great, old kingdoms of Africa, evidently knew well. It is also possible that, having attained a level of complex civilization, the moral, spiritual and intellectual capacity of peoples to identify new problems and to solve them will be stunted by false maps of reality, so that people will gradually revert to clan or tribal, ethnic or nationalist loyalties; they could maintain their communitarian solidarity by reducing expectations and closing off the transforming influence of high religion, cultural reach and complex civilizations—as evidently happened in many societies known only by their ruins.

The decisive issue to be faced is the struggle for meaning by which to interpret the now singular world. This is also a global struggle to define those forms of justice that can link the levels of humanity into covenants of mutual accountability and responsibility, shaping the corporate units by which the daily bread of all will be earned so that they, too, will manifest the highest degrees of justice possible in governing units of civilization. That will require theology for the formation of a new social ethic also for families, schools, the professions, and workers: nothing else can grasp the ultimate foundations on which a governing system for the whole can be guided. Nothing else reaches far enough beyond it. Nothing else exists solely to be a servant of that which alone can comprehend the whole, with nothing to gain.

Protestant Christianity presses the hierarchy of life toward equity. It is not egalitarian in the sense that everything and everyone is to be always treated as equal in all respects, but Christians do not easily tolerate a social situation in which some are so poor that they can only think about subsistence and can neither gain from nor contribute to the common good. Similarly, Christians are suspicious of those who are so wealthy that they do not have to think of others, or their distress. Central to the Christian ethic is sharing, compassion, and sacrifice for others—and a willingness to call everyone to their duties, to change their lives, to develop their gifts, to live rightly, and to judge them, with mercy, when they do not.

It is striking that the classic ethic of distribution is balanced by an equally profound, but recently less emphasized, ethic of production, and a stewardly concern for the formation of a civil society that make it possible. The early church studied the Hebrew scriptures to see how to conduct the economic life in obedience, compassion and prudence, and the ancient monks developed a striking teaching that the holy life consisted of prayer and work (*orare et laborare*). Protestant Christians believe that humans can and should participate, with a bowed head, in the transformation of the world to the glory of God and the service of all peoples. The nurturing of well-ordered families and of dedicated workers and professionals able to participate in just, productive, and efficient corporations may well be a part of the vocation of all believers in our times.[10]

Protestant Christianity has, more than any other religious movement in the past, developed the inner moral and spiritual resources to support just these aspects of life. It now faces the challenge of doing it again, on a more intentional and larger scale—taking on also the challenge of reconstructing our civil society at the local levels and reaching again toward a new missionary outreach that can aid the globe.

How Then Shall We Live?

Because many parts of Christianity have underestimated the theological importance of preparing people for responsible participation in the economic part of civil society, personally or institutionally, much of the discussion of ethical issues in this area is framed in non- or anti-theological terms. Many discussions of family life, medical ethics, education and ethics, morality in the media, and business ethics simply pay no attention to what religion has to say. Yet these discussions are increasing, because people want to know how to live in complex institutions.

It is not possible for the practically minded theologian, or the practicing clergy, to become an expert in all the areas that constitute modern complex societies. However, it is possible to become familiar with certain of the key debates that have begun to rage among non-theological specialists who work in this area. We should also note that these debates often are polarized into conflicting paradigms of what ethics is all about, and discover ways of putting these conflicts into perspective.

To do this, we must reach more deeply into the resources of the Protestant heritage and discover certain motifs and themes that both modulate, or even overcome, the reductionistic models that preoccupy many and prevent contemporary ethics from speaking clearly to our age. Let us take three examples.

Contextualism and Absolutism

In resistance to the formalistic and sometimes legalistic ways in which ethical principles are presented to people, and in rebellion against the rigid ways in which both ethical values are sometimes imposed, some argue that a contextual way of making moral decisions is appropriate for our times, and that we can stop hitting people over the heads with absolutes. Is it not true that moral guidelines derive from the specific contexts in which we live? Especially in regard to economic issues, the context of global interaction puts many questions well beyond the range of what any single culture would define as "right."

It is surely so that we should take particular contexts of life into account. What is proper in a boxing match is not proper in a marriage. But there is no evidence that being sensitive to contexts undercuts the importance or necessity of absolutes. Of course, it partly depends on how one defines "absolutes," and some contend that having absolutes means that one views ethics as a fixed loyalty to a standard of conduct which can be and must be applied to all people in all situations in exactly the same way. Such a definition is a convenient way of disposing of absolutes, for no known theory of ethics or law has ever said that.

Even the most rigorous jurist ruling under a rigorous legal system knows that at least three activities are required in every situation: coming to a finding of fact, coming to a finding of law, and combining these in a judgment which takes both into account. Contextual analysis, which allows the discernment of actual or important from apparent or unimportant facts, does not, in any sense, void the necessity of discerning also which parts or meanings of a law are to govern in the case. Nor, if contextual mitigating circumstances are taken into account in making the judgment, does it mean that the *principles* embodied in the law are de-absolutized or have to be applied in exactly the same way in all situations.

Protestant ethics, like most Christian ethics, requires coming to judgment by interpreting the context and weighing purported facts *and* by discerning what principles, values, or laws are of God, and thus will not dissolve in the changing tides of circumstance. Then, these have to be brought together in a decision, action, program, or policy. Protestants tend to join contextualists in protesting formalism and legalism, but they also protest every effort to make contextual conditions, or, for that matter, their own judgments, absolute. Therefore, the grace of justification through faith is required, precisely because they know that they live under absolutes not of their own making.

In addition, the contexts of life very often themselves can and should be judged by absolute principles, values, or laws that stand beyond the context. The presence, power, justice, and love of God may well be in every context of life, but in a world of sin, these are repressed, denied, or resisted. Protestants affirm that there is no defensible ethical reason to approve passivity in the face of alterable and unprincipled contexts. Absolutes external to the contexts provide the leverage to judge them.

Individualism and Community

Because Protestantism calls for people to come to judgments, it is often viewed as a highly individualistic tradition. There is some truth to that. Protestantism has a very high regard for each person, and sees each soul as made in the image of God, no matter how distorted life may be on the surface. And, just for this reason, Protestantism has long been a defender of human rights. The moral and spiritual dignity of a person ought not to be violated, even if what that person does fails to fulfill communally defined obligations or display virtue. Indeed, Protestants are mildly distrustful of too much talk of "virtue" in ethics, for very often it connotes two things that are put under suspicion in the most profound Protestant ethics.

First, most virtue ethics presume that within everyone is a natural inclination to the good. Protestants believe that while all are created good, everyone participates in the compromise of that goodness, so that we are inclined at least to a mixture of good and evil. Therefore, it is so difficult to be good without God, that the purely human habituation to virtue is unreliable. In fact, most Protestants hold that a conversion or a recognition that we are absolutely dependent on a

Reality beyond ourselves is necessary to steady and enable every resolve to be virtuous.

Second, most virtue theories argue that virtues are formed in the natural communities of which people are a part, and related to particular practices. That is how they get habituated, and this is what forms people who manifest the virtues. Protestants are surely interested in forming people who are trustworthy, and who not only show prudence, wisdom, justice, and courage, but are faithful, loving, and hopeful. Yet Protestants doubt that these virtues emerge from adhering to the habituated practices of natural communities. Natural communities are often ethnocentric, patriarchal, superstitious, violent, and plagued with disease and ignorance; they are often governed by traditional rules, roles, and relationships that make virtue possible only for some, or that swallow personal identity into group solidarities in ways that actively discourage virtue. Thus, Protestants seek to form associations of people called out of the natural communities.

The charge that Protestantism is individualistic turns out to be not entirely true. It does tend to break with, and thus to break up, natural communities; but it also immediately forms new associations and relationships that, if not "community" in the traditional sense, have structures of association marked by a demand for the human rights of each person, and a mutual accountability under principles to which they have given a personal assent and that are not merely the cultivated habits of a tradition. Further, this association—initially the gathered church, subsequently all sorts of organizations that restructure civilization—presses all toward what the World Council of Churches has called a "Responsible Society": a vision of an interdependent, federated system of associations, each having particular values, purposes, and ends that, like virtues, are particular to each practice, but which live under a common universal law and by mutual constraint.

Incentive and Opportunity

In all modern societies, and so far as we can see in future economies, it is clear that we shall have a sizable portion of the population who will live on the underside. They will be poor, sometimes elderly or ill, sometimes young and vulnerable, all ill-equipped to cope with the vast, complex society. Often these are those who have most recently had their natural communities shattered by change, either systemic (the shift to global interactions and federated associations) or more personal (an accident, a death, a divorce, an abandonment, a job loss, a flood).

The ethical debate about how to care for these people rages. One side calls for carrots and sticks to reduce dependency and force participation in the work and lifestyle of the new society; they may have to live at the very bottom of the economic ladder, but they must grasp the available rung to survive. This view sees the poor as people of potential, but underutilized, competence who must be pressed to take advantage of real, if limited, possibilities. The other side calls for compassionate support for people in trouble by directly providing them with the resources to live decently. One side sees the problem as rooted in the moral irresponsibility of those who refuse to constrain impulses and take advantage of real, if demanding, options that are available, because they can see an easier way—depending on government largess. The other side sees the problem as the victimization of people by systematic exclusion and lack of opportunity, which need to be remedied by government assistance to the disadvantaged.

The various strategies that are proposed to deal with this situation are faulty on both sides, for one sees the issue as one of individual incentives, the other as the failure of collective responsibility. The fault is on several counts. First, both tend to see the key actors in this situation as two—persons and government—and thus the issue is debated in terms of less or more government support for individuals (or, for individuals who are a part of an underprivileged group). Second, both tend to see the issue as essentially economic—one in terms of individual economic activity, and the other in terms individual economic opportunity. Third, they both tend to see economics as basically material in origin and result. It is more likely that we have an accumulation of multiple problems—personal, social, and spiritual problems—with religion at the core.

It is not at all clear how the present debate about "ending welfare as we know it" will come out, but it is unlikely that either of the present strategies will do much good. The reason is that some people are unlikely to respond in a creative way to incentives or offered opportunities, however they are packaged. Some are not able; some are not willing; some see no reason to live other than self-destructive lives. A small percentage in every society constitutes a criminal subculture that must be controlled by police power. Protestants are, for the most part, very doubtful that everyone can and will be saved from the powers of sin, and recognize that the humane treatment of the perpetually dependent, and the firm constraint of the perpetually crooked (by coercive force and incarceration where necessary), are proper Christian vocations. Further, a major percentage of the populations who are poor are likely to respond to incentives or opportunities only if and when they see a purpose in life and find a network of people who care about them and about whom they care. In other words, the most effective clue to the helping of this segment of the poor, at home or abroad, is to draw them into a deep and abiding commitment to the most powerful transformative force known to humanity, which we know in Jesus Christ, and to invite them into disciplined associations of commitment, to worship and praise that source of change. Evangelization, church planting, and mission remain the most powerful resources to fight poverty.

On the basis of such a transformation of values, and the cultivated ability to participate in and help organize the life of an association, people can build all sorts of associations for education, rehabilitation from vicious habits, family formation, child care and parenting training, artistic creativity, political empowerment, and legal advocacy. Especially in our time, technological access and the skills to form and sustain economic corporations connected to the global economy can be built. If public funds can help in this, so much the better; but recent political trends suggest that such support comes and goes and can easily be altered by all sorts of political contingencies. Whether or not the government supports such efforts, the churches must undertake a new reformation for our time from the inside out. They will not fulfill their vocation, help the poor, nurture a vibrant, pluralistic civil society, overcome the propensity of present policies to oscillate between collectivism and individualism if they only organize protest groups or only call on the government to act.

How then shall we live? We must enable people to interpret contexts in a way that invites also discovering first principles, and coming to judgment. We must seek the conversion of souls, bringing people to the recognition of their relation to a source beyond themselves; living in a covenanted association of people willing to leave natural communities will inspire and support virtuous habits and invite action toward a responsible society. And on these bases, we must care for the disabled and draw the poor into the building of the infrastructure for civil society. The faith and the church are the core of the true War on Poverty. The clergy who do these things are the most important resource of the future for the salvation of souls and civilization.

The Role of Politics in Reforming Ethics

What then shall we say politically as we move toward a revitalized Protestant ethics, one that does not see politics as the center of life or government as the comprehending social reality? This view does not denigrate responsible governmental action in the least. It does mean that political institutions must continue to maintain law and order, and that they also must move toward policies that support the forming and sustaining of a wide variety of institutions that have substantial independence from governmental control, that nurture responsible associations at the grass roots. Yet government should have very little to do directly with individuals through giant bureaucracies, and should facilitate the development of other, more vital, organizations. We shall want to see that public policy is supportive of families, a variety of educational institutions, the formation of wealth-creating corporations among disadvantaged people, as well as being open to the new international world in which we will encounter peoples of other cultures and religions.[11] The avoidance of inherited caste positions will surely also require the availability of health care protection for those with greatest needs and disabilities (even if current proposals seem unable to gain support), and effective anti-discrimination laws in all the structures of civil society that receive tax funds.

Just as important is the granting of greater resources to religiously sponsored organizations insofar as they develop effective schools, nursery care, anti-drug programs, job training, and parenting skills programs, distinct from the worshiping community. The common funding of religious-based social service agencies, possibly through voucher programs, would recognize that key changes in people's lives only come on a religious basis. Both at home, and in international mission programs, training in the skills needed to form and sustain corporations at the grass roots would be a great gift. There is no reason that everything must be done on a non-profit basis, although obviously some charitable functions can only be carried out on that basis. If public support for government social services is to be sustained, it will have to rest on values of compassion,

69

care, and practical wisdom built up by religious and ethical agencies beyond government itself.

Under the historic impact of the Social Gospel and Christian Realism, and of Protestantism's recent baptisms of liberationist, "Third World," and "Green" forms of monism, many contemporary Protestant leaders have become contemptuous of the corporation. I have already noted that the corporation, like the family and the state, or even organized religious groups, can become demonic. It can ride roughshod over persons and cultures; it can destroy the beauties of creation for the sake of gain; it can reduce every issue and principle to a calculation of profit; it can purchase its way out of legal accountability; it can exploit workers and corrupt governments and become an idolatrous temple for the mad pursuit of Mammon. It can, it has, and it likely will again do all these things—just as the family can become a locus of sexual exploitation, a center of egocentrism, a patriarchal center of abuse, and an obsessive, or a totemic substitute for a community of faith. Governments can become tyrannies, empires, a terror to the people, and the center of personality cults or militarism; indeed, church groups can become satanic, manipulative, pagan, secularized, exploitative, heretical, or idolatrous.

The fact of corruptibility in all human institutions does not, however, negate the possibility that precisely these worldly organizations can also become instruments of preservation and creativity. Indeed, they can become occasions of grace—concretely and in limited, material, and temporal ways: covenantal concretions of faithful, hopeful, and loving existence, bearing indications and hints of the promises toward which God may be moving the world in this period of globalization. If constitutional democracy under just law can be seen as a concrete blessing for government in our time, if a loving, co-archic, covenanted marriage can be a center of graciousness in our era, and if truly faithful, ecumenical churches can be a signal of the ultimate unity of the one triune God today and a witness to the laws, purposes, and calling of God among the people, it may be possible for forms of corporate life to be a theologically and ethically valid form of economic cooperation and production in this moment of world history.

It may even be that our current situation has revealed more clearly than ever before what may have always been the case: economic life is an independent order of God's creation, an aspect of God's providential care for humanity, and a potential locus for the promises of redemption. It has always been there. But it has been subsumed under the family life, and then it turns intimate human relationships into calculations of gain and structures of ownership. Or it has been seen as the function of government, and then it combines police and economic power in one set of hands. Or it has been seen as the basis for religious life, and then it tempts us to displace Christ with Mammon. The formation of the corporation as distinct from these institutions may bring to actuality as great a change for the economic sector of life, as constitutions did for democracy, the university did for education, and the hospital did for medicine. Each of these was deeply distrusted, and only gradually secured a place in the revised visions of what have been called "orders of creation," "mandates of preservation," or "spheres of relative sovereignty." The corporation too may come to be treated as an instrument of peace, justice, and equity, able to create resources for the common life.

That, of course, depends on how the corporation gets structured, and whether it incarnates fundamental moral and spiritual values that help sustain civil society. We already know that it takes production out of the hands of the family and of the state, where sexual calculation or power interests may distort the values that ought to be sovereign there, it draws individuals out of their economic isolation, and it establishes a sphere where economic matters are understood by all to be central, under internal and external constraints. If it is rightly formed, and open to constant, ethical reformation, the corporation may take its place with the family, the neighborhood, the school, the hospital, the law court and even the church as a potentially graceful center of human vocation and civil service.

The Protestant churches, and especially their leaders in the seminaries, the pulpits, and the denominational offices, have not yet come to recognize this possibility. Indeed, many are blinded to or convinced against this possibility. That, in turn, has allowed individualistic theories of capitalism and "free market" to falsely claim a victory over socialism, and to reign in the interpretations of what business leaders in the pews actually do in their lives. All this has made most of what church leaders say about economic life seem irrelevant and distorting.

When the corporation is rightly ordered, it can generate not only the resources to overcome poverty and dependency, but also on a larger scale a new array of international legal arrangements that demand the quest for inter-contextual definitions of justice. It can foster fresh patterns of cross-cultural cooperation and mutuality, and more universalistic modes of interaction than previous interpretations thought were possible. In several ways, humans are learning through the modern corporation to relate to one another in a wide variety of styles, situations, cultures and locales.

These developments have today brought us to a new, more direct encounter with the great world religions—especially Hinduism, Buddhism, Confucianism, and Islam—which represent the most important, powerful, and profound representations of alternative religious and ethical systems that have ever been able to form enduring civilizations.[12] These are much greater, and much more serious challenges to Christianity than fascism or communism precisely because they more nearly approximate the overt, principled universalism present in religious potentialities and have shown a capacity to organize large and enduring civilizations on these grounds.

I have already suggested the wider implications of this view: politics is no longer the chief organizing institution of this cosmopolitan world. This forces us to think not only of the end of Westphalia, but of the end of a long conversation between Christianity and the Greek philosophers on one hand and Roman rulers on the other, as well as the long parallel conversations between Confucianism and the emperor, the Brahmans and the Kshatrias, the Buddhist monks and royalty, and between Mohammed the Prophet and Mohammed the Conqueror.

It does not seem to be true that all Constantinian relations are a betrayal of all true theology. In fact, the United States may be facing a Constantinian challenge that we are less well prepared to face than some of the religio-political connections mentioned above. We shall be judged wanting by God and history if we do not face the fact that we are thrust into the role of the only remaining super-power, and that all that we do must be as much governed by the highest standards of justice and the widest vision of the common good. Our actions must be as practical for the lives of all people as humanly possible. Indeed, it is central to the social teachings of Protestantism that we must continue to be politically engaged and responsible, and see all we do in this area as under God's sovereign and never-closing eye.

Yet the reality of politics even in this situation is being reduced in importance, even superseded—perhaps only for a time—by new economic relationships. Political leaders already are evaluated on the basis of how well they help the economy; it is quite possible that whatever we attempt to do in the future will be influenced by corporations, which not only are the chief bearers and generators of technology but the chief sources of jobs, wealth, and hope for material well-being. If they or families or churches fail, civil society will also fail, and many people will die as a result.

Come, Let Us Reason Together

I have no doubt that some people for whom I have regard will disagree with what is contained here. Some will say that this is nothing new, and I agree. Others will wonder whether all aspects are faithful to the prophetic traditions of Christian teaching; certainly I intend such fidelity. The essay is intended to evoke, even provoke, a renewal of Protestant thought about economic life and of Christian social ethics more broadly. At least it calls for a renewed examination of where we have been and where we are going, of what we should stand against and what we may stand for. Even more, it asks Whom we stand under, as we think, learn, and teach about these matters in a new global situation.

It does seem that if Protestantism does not undertake fresh and frank conversations on these matters, its great gifts to the world could fade. We still have to face Paul Tillich's question, posed early in the century, as to whether we are at "the end of the Protestant era." Some say now that, given the reforms of Vatican II in the Roman Catholic tradition, or given the sad state of the theology and ethics in many "mainline" churches, the answer must be in the affirmative. I do not believe that is so. The vibrant growth of Evangelical and Pentecostal churches among the world's emerging middle and poorer classes is less a terror to be feared than a lesson to be learned. It is also true that Protestants can find much in contemporary Catholic life and teaching to applaud, as already mentioned, and surely ecumenical Protestants can join with many Evangelicals and most Roman Catholics on many common issues. We share more, at deeper levels, than we differ on the surface. But Protestants would fail to be faithful stewards, before God and humanity, of what we have been given— thereby condemning not only parts of the world, but ourselves to damnable memory—if we did not engage in reforming the enduring features of Protestant social ethics for a global era, as a "challenge-gift" for all. To that end this volume, and this series, hopes to contribute.

Chapter 2

Vice and Virtue in Economic Life

Peter L. Berger

The title of this essay contains an instructive ambiguity. "Vice" and "virtue" are, of course, terms that come out of ethical discourse. They refer in this context to the realm of experience in which judgments about right and wrong, good and evil, are made. In the context of economic life, however, it is possible to use these same terms in a way that is morally neutral, or at least ethically attenuated. For instance, one might say that the cardinal virtue in any business is to know its market niche, while a major vice is to produce goods or services for which there is no market. Such a statement refers primarily to the logic of market economics, with only indirect ethical implications. There is little intrinsically immoral in producing a product that no one wants to buy, although it may be wrong to be wasteful of resources; and conversely there is no intrinsic moral status vested in market research, even if it is good to discern and serve the neighbor's needs. In other words, moral judgments and statements of economic logic may have overlapping implications, but they may also belong to discrete universes of discourse. In this, of course, economic life is by no means unique. Thus an engineer can make morally neutral statements about bridge construction, while the moralist may praise or condemn the uses to which this bridge is intended to be put. More broadly, then, it is possible analytically to separate statements of how the world works from statements on how human beings should behave in the world.

When it comes to economic life, there are indeed cases where its own logic happily coincides with the imperatives of morality. Thus a number of historians have argued that the industrial revolution made serfdom and slavery economically dysfunctional, since free labor employed for wages was less costly than the paternalistic maintenance required by the earlier forms of unfree labor. The moralist, who has condemned serfdom or slavery for reasons that have nothing to do with economics, may then rejoice that here is a case where virtue has its own reward (or, to use an American colloquialism, where it is possible to do well by doing good). This coincidence between ethical and economic virtue, however, is not to be expected in all cases—indeed, very probably it is the exception rather than the rule. For example, a major economic problem in advanced industrial societies today is overstaffing. Economic logic suggests enterprises that are "lean and mean," relying increasingly on technology rather than human labor. Globalization has meant that labor-intensive activities are increasingly shifted from the advanced to the developing economies. The result of this, of course, has been chronic (so-called structural) unemployment in the advanced economies, affecting especially the unskilled and low-skilled sectors of the labor force. The economic virtue here is in sharp conflict with moral considerations concerning, say, the dignity and the rights of middle-aged workers in the manufacturing industry who are difficult if not impossible to retrain for jobs in the high-technology/capital-intensive activities in which economies like that of the United States can successfully compete globally. For another example, a major economic problem in industrial democracies is the aging of the population: more and more old people burden the welfare state that must be supported by a shrinking group of younger, economically productive people. Economic logic suggests the progressive curtailing of benefits to the aged, including the "rationing" of medical care (a euphemism for the denial of services) and the legalization of "assisted suicide" (a euphemism, one has reason to fear, for involuntary demise). It is not only older people with paranoid proclivities (such as the author of this essay) who can foresee a time when the practices of these societies will resemble those of traditional Eskimo culture, where old people were set adrift on leaky rafts to perish in the icy sea. One hopes that it will not only be older people who will perceive a certain moral problem in such a situation.

This incongruence between ethical and economic rationales will have to be taken up again toward the end of this essay. It is important, however, to keep it in mind all along. It is all too often overlooked in the discussion of economic strategies, where one possible course of action is called "good," another "bad." The arrogant prescriptions for economic policy made by economic experts all the time in the Third

World and in the formerly Communist societies offer an instructive if depressing illustration of a concept of "the good" antiseptically segregated from moral considerations.

All the same, having said this, the present argument can focus on the economic logic of different societal situations in strictly analytic terms. This means that, for the moment, ethical questions can be shelved. (The engineer can do the same as he explains the problems of constructing a certain bridge, postponing for the moment the moral judgment as to whether this bridge is to be used to invade a neighboring country or to transport food to a starving region; for either purpose, the analytic problems of bridge-construction will be the same.) It is equally important to understand that, *even in terms of strict economic logic*, matters of moral motivation, or of "values" (in current parlance), cannot be ignored. The reason for this is actually very simple: while the analyst can shelve questions of morality, the acting person out there in the real world usually does not. Put differently, the moral beliefs and practices of economic actors inevitably affect their behavior, and therefore affect the functioning of the economy within which they act. Put differently again, actions that might be deemed "irrational" in strictly economic terms can be highly "rational" in terms of the moral motivations of living individuals. Vilfredo Pareto, the great Italian economist writing in the early part of this century, came to this conclusion and found it necessary to invent a discipline that he called "sociology" in order to explain the "non-logical" actions that, he thought, constituted the larger part of human activity overall. It is ironic that many economists have still not learned this lesson, being surprised over and over again that people refuse to behave in the way that economic theory says they must behave.

Any discussion of the relation between moral values and economic life evokes the mighty ghost of Max Weber. It will soon be a century since Weber published his famous essay on *The Protestant Ethic and the Spirit of Capitalism*, over which there still rages a lively debate among historians and social scientists. As is well known, Weber believed that the moral consequences of the Protestant Reformation, especially in its Calvinist wing, were an important factor in the genesis of modern capitalism in Europe and North America. Subsequently, most of Weber's gigantic opus dealt with the relations of religion, morality, and economic life in premodern and non-Western societies, ranging from the ancient Near East and classical antiquity to the cultures of South and East Asia. In each case, Weber tried to understand how religious traditions shaped moral systems, and how the latter in turn helped or hindered various economic developments. It is not necessary to agree with all or even most of Weber's statements on these relationships in order to agree with his basic approach. In other words, one need not accept Weber's answers in order to accept his questions. In this sense, and in this sense only, the presuppositions of this essay are "neo-Weberian."

It is, again, in this sense that the present author and his colleagues at Boston University have been exploring questions of "economic culture." That term itself is, if you will, "neo-Weberian." It simply refers to the cultural context within which, inevitably, economic activity takes place. It does not assume *a priori* that there is any particular relation between culture and economic life, certainly not that culture always and onesidedly determines economic activities; it only assumes that there *is* a relation, the exact nature of which must be investigated empirically in each instance. The concept of "culture" here is the conventional one as employed in the social sciences. It refers to the sum of beliefs, values, and lifestyles in any group of human beings. As such, the concept embraces more than morality; however, necessarily, it always includes morality.

While the specific relationship between culture and economic life must be studied empirically in any given case, it is possible to say that typically the two complexes of human meanings and activity interact in a reciprocal manner, rather than one simply determining the other. There are cases of the latter sort of relationship. The advent of a cultural phenomenon, such as a religious movement of great charismatic fervor, may radically change economic behavior. If Weber was right, this is precisely what certain versions of Protestantism did in the seventeenth and eighteenth centuries. Conversely, an economic innovation may have drastic effects on culture, even transforming it completely. The effect of modern industry on traditional European village cultures may be an example of the second type of relationship. In these instances, culture and economics are, respectively, in the role of causal dominance or independent variable, with the other complex being respectively acted upon as dependent variable. But these, if you will, hammer-and-anvil situations are relatively rare. More common, the two complexes interact in a less unidirectional manner. Culture modifies economic life, as economic life modifies culture. The precise manner in which either modification occurs is open to empirical inquiry. The findings of such inquiry are usually as practically useful (as to the business person or the policy maker) as they are intellectually interesting (usually to every sort of social scientist *except* economists).

Max Weber described the Protestant ethic, to which he ascribed this major historical role in the genesis of the modern market economy, as an "inner-worldly asceticism" (*innerweltliche Askese*; the German phrase has also been translated more liberally as "this-worldly asceticism"). By this he meant the following: this was a morality that was ascetic in that it idealized self-denial and discipline. To that extent, the Protestant ethic had certain similarities with the ethic of Roman Catholic monasticism—think of the classical Benedictine discipline of *orare et laborare*, prayer and work.. But unlike the monastic ethic, Protestantism focused its attention on *this* world, idealizing the responsible exercise of wordly vocations from that of the prince to that of the washer woman. The theological grounding of this turn from other-worldly to this-worldly concerns, and the consequent paradoxical relation between Protestantism and secularization, cannot be pursued here (fascinating those these topics are). What must be emphasized is that, strictly in terms of economic logic, this Protestant ethic (always assuming that Weber's thesis is historically valid) was highly *functional* during the nascent period of modern capitalism and the ensuing industrial revolution. One would always be tempted to paraphrase Voltaire by saying that, if Protestantism had not existed, it would have had to be invented.

Weber was also quite clear as to *why* there was this "affinity" (his term was *Wahlverwandschaft*) between Protestant this-worldly asceticism and early capitalism. At this stage of economic development what is needed are, first, entrepreneurs animated by a spirit of rational risk-taking and profit-making for reinvestment rather than lavish consumption—and, second, a growing labor force that is disciplined and amenable to training. The Protestant ethic provided (or, if you will, legitimated) all these virtues. It encouraged disciplined application to whatever one's work happened to be, it inculcated a modest lifestyle (thus encouraging the "primitive accumulation" of capital needed for economic growth), and, last but not least, its positive attitude to education for the laity fostered an increasingly skilled labor force. Given these facts, it is not surprising that the Protestant (and especially the Calvinist and Calvinist-influenced) regions of Europe and North America came to be in the vanguard of both the capitalist and the industrial transformations of the modern world. One can go beyond this historical proposition and hypothesize that an ethic of this-worldly asceticism, with just these characteristics, is a functional requirement of modern economic take-off at any time and in any society, irrespective of the ideas (religious or other) by which such an ethic is legitimated. This thought has led a number of analysts (the Israeli sociologist Shmuel Eisenstadt is prominent among them) to look for "functional equivalents" of the Protestant ethic in various cultures around the world today. The reasoning here is that the original push into modern economic activity from a premodern situation (be it marked by feudalism or some other socioeconomic system) requires people given to hard work, discipline, delayed or frugal consumption, and a readiness to accept rationalizing innovations. Conversely, people with a culture (which, let it be said, could be very attractive) of easy-going enjoyment of the moment, lack of regimentation, lavish festivities, and loyalty to traditions however irrational economically, are unlikely to be successful candidates for a modern economic take-off.

It so happens that, however useful the search for "functional equivalents" of the Protestant ethic, it is unnecessary to support the aforementioned hypothesis on required economic virtues. For there is going on today, in much of the world, a gigantic Protestant revival that replicates to an uncanny degree the dynamics described by Max Weber in an earlier period. This is the rapid spread of Evangelical Protestantism (most of it Pentecostal in form) in vast areas of the Third World—in East and Southeast Asia (notably in South Korea, in all the Chinese societies, in the Philippines, as well as in the Pacific archipelago), in Africa south of the Sahara, and most spectacularly throughout Latin America. (Indeed, the only non-Western regions unaffected by this Protestant explosion are the Muslim countries, South Asia and, curiously, Japan.) Undoubtedly there are different reasons for this religious development, and they will vary from country to country. But it can be proposed with some assurance that here is a moral system that will be peculiarly attractive to people caught in the cauldron of modernization and that will be peculiarly functional in supplying the virtues likely to be rewarded in this situation. Despite a number of significant differences from earlier Protestant movements (the Pentecostal style of worship is an important one), the *moral* content is amazingly similar. One may say that Max Weber is alive and well, and living in Guatemala.

David Martin, in a recent study,[1] has provided a rich description of what is in effect a cultural revolution. He posits that "new" Protestants (the spectacular growth of Protestantism in Latin America did not begin until after World War II) are transforming some of the most deeply rooted characteristics of their traditional culture. That culture was consumption- rather than production-oriented, it was anything but ascetic, it was hedonistic and not greatly enamored of discipline, and it was tradition-bound to the neglect of innovation. The new Protestant ethic, just like the old one to the north, inculcates diametrically opposed values and lifestyles—disciplined work, delayed gratification, planning for the future, entrepreneurial innovation—in sum, all the virtues conducive to what Weber called "rationalization." Protestantism weakens and in some areas liquidates the traditional Latin American *compadre* system, since it takes away the Roman Catholic practices around which that system was constructed: No more confirmation and first communion, thus much less of a need for *compadres*—and, perhaps even more important, in many branches of this new Protestantism, no more infant baptism. It has been argued that it is just this *compadre* system that has been an obstacle to economic success—because it legitimates the claims of many people to participate in even the most modest capital accumulation by an individual, and because it necessitates a large number of expensive *fiestas*; both these characteristics discourage savings and investment in favor of immediate consumption. Probably the most dramatic revolution has been the anti-*machismo* thrust of the new Protestantism. The Protestant movement, to an astounding degree, is driven by women. While most of the preachers are men, the evangelists and the organizers are mostly women, many of them formidable women indeed. With not too much exaggeration, one could even describe the new Protestantism as a women's movement. What then happens is that these women "domesticate" their menfolk—no more drinking, no more gambling, no more sex "on the side" (what in Mexico is called the institution of the *casa chica*), no more lavish entertainment of "the boys." And if the men refuse this "domestication," they are eventually thrown out.

The economic consequences of this behavioral metamorphosis are beginning to be evident. Not everywhere: There are areas in Latin America (for example, in southern Mexico or in the *nordeste* of Brazil) where the macroeconomic situation is so bad that the behavior of individuals, at least in the poorer classes, makes little difference—

Protestant or Catholic, hard-working or easy-going, ascetic or hedonistic, most people remain stuck in poverty. But in areas of the continent where there has been significant economic development, it is becoming visible that practitioners of the neo-Protestant ethic have what could well be called a comparative advantage. Chile is a notable case in point. As is well-known by now, since the economic reforms of the Pinochet regime Chile has experienced a sustained economic take-off, with beneficent consequences for almost all sectors of the population. For large numbers of Chileans there are now real possibilities of an exit from poverty. Given this macroeconomic fact, the behavior of individuals makes a difference. Thus one can see in Chile the beginnings of a Protestant middle class, a phenomenon with vast social and political as well as economic implications.

Here, then, is a textbook case of a charismatic religious movement creating a new culture, virtually *ex nihilo*, which in turn has far-reaching consequences in terms of economic behavior. But charismatic religious revolutions are by no means the only cases in which culture influences economics. There are also cases of centuries-old cultural traits which, in a new situation, suddenly produce unanticipated economic effects.

The meteoric rise of the economies of East and Southeast Asia in the post-World War II period has given rise to one of the more interesting discussions of economic culture. Japan is the key for this discussion—the first non-Western country to successfully modernize itself, already more than a century ago as a result of the Meiji Restoration and then with amazing dynamism after 1945. But, of course, Japan is no longer alone as an Asian "economic miracle." There were then the "four little dragons"—South Korea, Taiwan, Hong Kong, and Singapore. More recently, the same economic dynamism has powerfully penetrated into much of Southeast Asia, notably Thailand, Malaysia, and Indonesia, and now also beginning in Vietnam (significantly, in all these countries the Chinese ethnic minority plays a disproportionately large role in the economy). Most recently, as a result of the far-reaching moves toward a market economy, mainland China (or at least large areas within China) is producing a gigantic "miracle" of its own, with potentially enormous consequences for the global economy. Invidious comparisons with other areas of the Third World—in other regions of Asia, in Africa and in Latin America—could not be avoided. While it is clear that the economic upsurge in eastern Asia was caused by a variety of factors, some of them having little or nothing to do with culture (such as market-friendly government policies, overall political stability, an entry into international trade under favorable conditions, and others), it was plausible to ask whether there were not also cultural factors that, minimally, helped along these economic developments.

A much-discussed answer to this question has been the "Post-Confucian hypothesis." Based on the observation that most of these societies have been strongly influenced by Confucian morality, the hypothesis is that this morality was, to say the least, an important causal factor in bringing about the aforementioned economic success stories. Put simply, Confucian morality could be seen as a "functional equivalent" of Weber's Protestant ethic, like the latter promoting virtues with a marked affinity to the requirements of modern economic take-off. This morality, like Protestantism, promoted a this-worldly asceticism, valuing hard work, discipline, self-denial/delayed gratification, saving over against quick consumption, positive attitudes toward entrepreneurship and education, and in addition acceptance of authority and hierarchy making for political stability.

There have been criticisms of this emphasis on Confucianism. For one thing, Confucianism in its full sense has been the cultural property of a small elite, while these economic developments were carried by large numbers of people, many of them barely literate, who would be blissfully ignorant of the Confucian classics. Also, other moral and religious traditions are possible candidates for the role of "functional equivalents"—Buddhism in various forms, Shinto, possibly Taoism, and certainly "folk religion" which everywhere in the region forms the cultural subsoil out of which the "great traditions" have grown. Be this as it may, there are cultural commonalities throughout the region; these can be ascribed to the broad dominance of Sinitic civilization, and Confucianism almost certainly is at least an important component of this cultural constellation (not necessarily in its classical "high" forms, but in the form of what Robert Bellah has nicely called "bourgeois Confucianism"). One could then say that these traits constitute a sort of "comparative cultural advantage" over against populations shaped by traditions less functional in a period of modern economic take-off.

A very instructive case in point is the economic culture of the Overseas Chinese—that is, the fifty or so millions of ethnic Chinese living outside the borders of the People's Republic. As already mentioned, these people are playing a strategic economic role far out of proportion to their actual numbers in many of the relevant societies. Gordon Redding, in his magisterial book *The Spirit of Chinese Capitalism*,[2] has provided a vivid picture of this economic culture (the allusion to Weber's famous essay was, of course, intentional). Here is a culture characterized by this-worldly realism, hard-nosed pragmatism, an immense capacity for disciplined hard work and ascetic self-denial, and a quick-minded flexibility in perceiving and acting upon entrepreneurial opportunity. A key role in this culture is played by the Chinese family—not in the conservative "extended-family" form characteristic of traditional China, but in the much more "nuclear" form as it developed in the Chinese diaspora. It is clear that this family functions in a very different way from, for example, the traditional Latin American (or, for that matter, African) family. While the latter manifests itself economically as mainly a community of shared consumption and thus as a brake on individual upward mobility, the Overseas Chinese family has turned itself into a community of shared production—a mix of migration-assistance agency, employment agency, investment and credit union, and, most important, a community of trust extending beyond countries and even continents. The typical economic unit that has emerged from this culture has been the Chinese family firm, an enormously vibrant and flexible economic actor (very different, incidently, from the much-described Japanese firm, which does not have this peculiar relation to kinship).

The case of the Overseas Chinese is useful in explicating two concepts relevant to the present topic. One, already mentioned, is that of "comparative culture advantage"; the other is that of "cultural latency."

The concept of "comparative cultural advantage" simply means that people having certain cultural traits—certain virtues, if you will—will have an economic advantage over people who don't. It is important to emphasize that this advantage is always relative. Thus, it is clearly not the case that Chinese people will always succeed economically, or that others can never hope to compete with them, or that quite different cultural traits may under certain circumstances also turn out to be economically functional (interesting instances of the last possibility are present efforts in Indonesia and Malaysia to enlist Islamic values in the service of modern economic development). Most important, the concept also implies that the advantage may be temporary; what was a "virtue" at one moment of economic history may turn out to be a "vice" at another. Thus Overseas Chinese economic culture favored small, flexible firms, with all key positions occupied by close relatives. The smallness was dictated by the limits of the community of trust: Since one can trust only close relatives, the firm cannot expand to the point where one runs out of individuals. There are important areas of economic activity, however, where larger, more complex organizations are required. Here the Chinese entrepreneurs are at a distinct *dis*advantage vis-à-vis the Japanese, who have had a genius for creating large organizations based on the loyalty of employees who are not related to each other by kinship ties. The Japanese case, however, also illustrates the relative, potentially temporary character of any cultural advantage. Modern Japan has created a highly collectivistic, conformist, non-individualistic culture. The Japanese themselves have called this a culture of "groupism"—the individual deriving meaning and identity from group membership. The role of this "groupism" in the culture of the Japanese corporation has been much studied, and indeed held up as an ideal to be emulated by non-Japanese management mavens. It is quite possible, though, that this economic culture was very functional in an era of early industrialization and mass manufacturing. It may be much less functional, possibly even definitely dysfunctional, in an era of knowledge-driven, high-technology and service-oriented economics. This new era might require a spirit of individualism and non-conformity that is quite alien to Japanese culture.

The concept of "cultural latency" refers to the fact that cultural traits that have been around for a long time may suddenly, as a result of changed circumstances, bring about totally unanticipated effects (economically or otherwise). This concept helps to answer the obvious question why Confucian morality (to stick to the hypothesis for a moment) has never before had the economic consequences for which it has been given credit in recent times. The Confucian virtues (as Weber, among others, pointed out) had a positively conservative function in traditional China. As the property of the Mandarin class (Weber's "literary bureaucrats"), this ethic was quite antagonistic to any economic activity. Merchants and traders, grubby chasers after profit who lacked refinement and self-cultivation, carried out occupations far below the dignity of a Confucian scholar-gentleman. Thus traditional China could not create the context for modern capitalism (Weber was quite right about this). And, obviously, there also could not be such a context in Communist China, before the

85

recent reinterpretation of Communist ideology, so as to legitimate the market economy (which has been the undoubted achievement in mental acrobatics of the regime of Deng Xiao Peng). But in the circumstances of the Chinese diaspora—in Taipei, Hong Kong, Jakarta, and indeed San Francisco or Honolulu—far from the constraints of Mandarins or of the extended family, and far from what Marx so eloquently called the "idiocy of village life"—suddenly old moral maxims took on a dynamism that no one could have foreseen in the old days or in the old country. In other words, cultural traits that, economically speaking, were "latent" or dormant for centuries, suddenly "woke up" to meet new needs and to open new possibilities of economically functional activities.

If there are "virtues" of production, what about consumption? When a society has reached a certain level of prosperity, are the old values still functional? This is not a new problem, of course. Observers of human events have long noted that prosperity makes for a softening of older, sterner forms of morality, a decline in belief and lifestyles of self-indulgence. The old notion of "decadence" neatly sums up these observations, probably more or less valid across a broad spectrum of human history. Specifically, "decadence" means the weakening of the firm moral convictions, a reluctance toward discipline, hard work, and self-denial, and the cultivation of a more refined, hedonistic way of life. The notion of "decadence" has further implied that societies going in this direction become easy prey for hardier people set on conquest. Thus "decadence" has been seen as, typically, the stage just before societal demise.

The interesting question that arises here is whether "decadence" will necessarily mean the same for an advanced industrial society as it has meant for premodern societies; this question will be taken up in a moment. But be this as it may, it is evident that prosperity in modern times has also led, if not to "decadence" right away, to a softening of the harsher morality of earlier times. As the countries animated by the Protestant ethic became more affluent, their culture remained this-worldly but it also became much less ascetic. The harsh self-denial of the "founding" era gave way to a much greater indulgence in luxury and easy living. A recent book by Colin Campbell makes a good argument for such a softening occurring in Protestant Europe in the seventeenth and eighteenth centuries at the hands of Romanticism.[3] Campbell also suggests, persuasively, that such a modification of Protestant morality was an economic necessity: As the modernizing economies produced more, *someone* had to be motivated to consume all these new products. That "someone," it turns out, is the same bourgeoisie that had initiated the revolution in production of early industrial capitalism.

Whatever may have happened in the past, there has been a significant cultural shift in Western societies since the late 1960s. This cannot be the place for a discussion of the causes of this development, nor of its numerous social and political consequences. But the following curious aspect of the matter must interest us here: Initially, the new cultural *gestalt* was, in its own term, a "counter-culture," a rebellion against bourgeois culture in general and against the values of the Protestant ethic in particular. It embraced pleasure and self-realization against hard work and discipline (in the apt phrases of Californian English, "hanging loose" against being "uptight"). It posited rebellion and spontaneity against the alleged repressions of "the system," a term that was broader than, but certainly inclusive of, the economic structures of modern capitalism. Now, in the decades since this cultural eruption, its major themes have been absorbed into the mainstream culture and even become part of an established orthodoxy (this is particularly the case with those themes in the counter-culture dealing with sexuality and reproduction). What is very interesting indeed is the way in which many of the same themes have infiltrated the very economic institutions that had been anathematized earlier, that is, the institutions of the capitalist business world.

There is a widespread new ideal of a "kinder, gentler" capitalism. It is difficult to determine just how widespread it is, since it is difficult to distinguish genuinely new conceptions of how to do business from public-relations rhetorics. Also the degree to which this idea is realized in business practice will obviously vary with overall economic conditions: A business can more readily afford to be "kinder, gentler" in good times than during a recession. There is enough evidence, though, to say that the business world in the United States and in Western Europe has taken in a good many ideas and practices that derive from the counter-culture. Ideologically, feminism, environmentalism, and multiculturalism are central to the process of cultural absorption. The corresponding practices would include affirmative action, programs to prevent "sexual harassment," "environment-friendly" modifications of manufacturing and other technical processes, "diversity management," and the like. Some of these innovations, of course, are moves made necessary by legislation and government regulation, and by the desire to avoid litigation. But it is plausible that the motives on the part of management are at least to some degree based on the conviction that these innovations are good in themselves. The notion of the "socially responsible corporation" embodies many of these ideas and practices. Possibly even more significant is the recent proliferation of "personal development programs" (PDP's) as a new concept of employee benefits and management training. Here the corporation offers a panoply of social and therapeutic services that go far beyond the conventional understanding of employee benefits. These include on-site day care, "elder care" (for the aged parents of employees), programs against alcohol and drug abuse and smoking, classes on proper exercise and dieting, and psychological counseling in various areas not related to the job. For higher management echelons this new ethos includes courses and weekend retreats that can aptly be described as programs of spiritual formation (some of them imported from Asia). In its full-blown version (which probably is, still, relatively rare) this would constitute the reshaping of the corporation into a "caring" institution, a sort of private-sector incarnation of the welfare state— the "nanny corporation," as Laura Nash has nicely called it (see her forthcoming volume in this series).

Now, it can also be said that these developments, occurring at the very heart of corporate capitalism, are an incorporation of "late-sixties" values at the expense of the old virtues of the business ethos as derived, ultimately, from the Protestant ethic. If the latter virtues could be described as rather *macho*, the word "feminization" might apply to the new constellation. Needless to say, these counter-cultural themes do not enter unchanged into this symbiosis with the business ethos. Just as they change the business culture, they are in turn changed by incorporation within it. This can be seen graphically if one looks at the individuals employed in these new programs. Most of them are youngish or early middle-aged practitioners of the "caring professions," many of them with a background of left-leaning political activism. As they become corporate functionaries or independent business consultants, they must change not only their appearance but some of their ideas. A kind of bargain is struck. The business world accepts and rewards many of the values that originated in the counter-culture—*except*, obviously, those that repudiated capitalism and all its works. The former counter-cultural types in turn surrender their wilder revolutionary ideas and "clean up their act," behaviorally as well as ideologically, to the degree necessary for them to operate successfully in the corporate milieu. This has some rather comical features, brought out well in two recent studies of these developments.[4] The comedy cuts both ways: the allegedly hard-bitten executive who speaks in the language of sensitivity and compassionate concern; and the former radical, still sporting a long coiffure and bumper stickers of vaguely revolutionary import, who charges exorbitant fees for his services to business and manages an income appropriate for middle-level executives.

In the language of the latter type's younger years, one could ask who is "co-opting" whom in this process. The question is probably meaningless. The bargain entails a synthesis, which could be interpreted in only seemingly contradictory ways. On the one hand, one could see this process as an undermining of the moral basis of capitalism, the "long march through the institutions" (Antonio Gramsci's famous phrase) having finally reached the very heart of the capitalist beast, which it will eventually destroy. On the other hand, the same process could be seen as yet another manifestation of the immense adaptability of modern capitalism, which can turn to its own profit almost anything, even ideas and movements that set out as its sworn enemies. "Decadence" on the one hand, creative adaption on the other: Perhaps the process is best understood as a bit of both. The question that suggests itself, though, is whether this new type of capitalism, if it should really come to characterize the economic culture of the Western democracies, will help or hinder the place of the latter in a highly competitive global economy.

To illustrate this point, an anecdote might serve. Some years ago I was asked to address a conference of Japanese businessmen. Having recently read a history of ancient Rome, I told the following story. In the early years of the Roman Republic, when it was constantly at war with the Greek kingdoms in southern Italy, an envoy of the Senate was sent to one of these Greek courts. One must imagine him as an uncomplicated, robust type, an embodiment of all the old Roman virtues. At dinner he found himself next to an Epicurean philosopher, who went on at length about the view of his philosophical school to the effect that the purpose of human life is happiness. The Roman envoy had never heard anything like this. He listened very attentively. When the Greek philosopher had finished his exposition, the envoy only said: "I hope that you will continue to hold these beliefs as long as you are at war with Rome." I drew the lesson for my Japanese audience by suggesting that a Japanese businessman looking at the culture of the contemporary West might well say: "I hope that you will continue to hold these beliefs as long as you are in competition with us." Now, some years later, I would be more doubtful about the implied hypothesis of this comment.

What is this hypothesis? It is, if you will, a "Protestant" one. The Roman envoy, of course, was implying a theory of decadence in his comment: the hedonistic ethos advocated by the Epicurean philosopher must necessarily undermine the martial virtues by which one prevails in war, thus giving Rome an advantage over their effete adversaries. In the event, he was right (and he would be proven right again centuries hence, when the barbarians from the north had a similar advantage over a Roman world that had similarly traded its old virtues for a hedonistic ethos). The lesson at the Japanese conference implied a similar advantage of the hard-nosed over the sensitive in the contest of international economic competition. However, this analogy can be questioned. It is not only that other than "Epicurean" values are still held on to by large groups of people in the West, and it is not only that the Japanese and other Asians, having attained high levels of affluence, seem to be influenced by all the putatively decadent Western values and lifestyles. More important to the present topic is this reflection: the "Protestant" virtues that were functional in an earlier period of Western economic development may no longer be functional today. On the contrary, it may well be that the economic activities with which the West can still be globally competitive now cannot only accommodate but may actually *require* the values and practices which the business world has been importing from the erstwhile counter-culture. In other words, the "caring" professions might well be earning their fees.

Add this further thought: In an advanced industrial economy, as a result of the immense productivity of its technology, a relatively small percentage of the total population can keep the basic productive machinery going. Suppose that this minority may still have to be animated by some approximation of the Protestant ethic—that is, by a more or less ascetic ethic of production. The system will reward their hard work in a commensurate financial manner. The great majority, though, is engaged in activities that simply do not require this degree of dedication. What is required—*economically* required, that is—of this majority is not so much an ethic of production but an ethic of consumption. In other words, "Epicureanism" may actually be just what is needed. This may not be a morally uplifting picture (Aldous Huxley, who drew a very similar picture in his *Brave New World*, thought that it was a nightmare). Even so, it may be precisely what the logic of this particular phase of economic history demands.

The argument of the preceding pages can be summed up quite succinctly in terms of two propositions. One: What is virtue, economically speaking, in one period of economic development may be vice in another, and vice versa. Two: There are virtues conducive to production in earlier phases of modern economic take-off; these will have to be replaced, at least in part, by virtues conducive to consumption in a later phase. The first proposition can be put forth with a good measure of confidence. The second, given the nature of the evidence, can only be stated as a hypothesis, subject to empirical disconfirmation. However, for the sake of the present argument, it is useful to consider it for its ethical implications on the assumption that it is indeed valid.

Quite apart from the ethical assessments one may wish to make of the two moralities, it is not difficult to see the human pain and even tragedy that such a succession of moral codes must bring about. Of course, this would not be the first time in history that one generation, for whatever reasons, comes to reject the moral principles of earlier generations. One aspect of this process that is novel, though, is the acceleration in such moral shifts. What in earlier times might have been a gradual change spanning several generations, today occurs much more quickly, very often from one generation to its immediate successor. This means, quite simply, and brutally, that children reject the morality of their parents. Take one of the cases earlier in this essay. Here are these new Protestants in Latin America, busily realizing their new ethic in a flurry of religious, social, and economic activism, to the neglect of much of the cultural heritage in their background. What must their parents feel? Very probably, a good deal of sorrow. It is not just the question of these children falling away from their ancestral faith; many Latin Americans are only nominally Catholic, so that aspect will not trouble everyone in the older generation. Much more painful will be the abandonment of so much else that traditionally had been part and parcel of a way of life—the roles of men and women in the family as well as in the larger world, the warmth and extended kinship and *compadre* ties, the cycle of festivities and sociability surrounding them, generally a relaxed manner of living one's life. Compared to this, many of these parents must think, the new Protestant lifestyle seems cold, frenetic, indeed perverse: have these young people gone mad, to live like this?

Take another case: Imagine a family of Chinese immigrants, somewhere in the United States. The parents spend their entire life in unrelenting hard work, perhaps running a restaurant or a laundry (two traditional Chinese entry-level occupations in America) seven days a week from early morning to late at night, never taking a vacation, spending very little. As a result of all this work and frugality, there are savings, most of them spent on the education of the children. Very often the result of these efforts is a big intergenerational jump in social mobility—the sons and daughters of such parents becoming professionals or executives. As they pass through higher education and enter new social worlds far removed from the parental milieu, they will inevitably absorb many if not the bulk of the values established among the people with whom they now associate. Many of these values will be the opposite of the parental asceticism—values of the hedonistic, consumption-oriented ethic described earlier. What must the parents feel? Will they feel like fools, having slaved away their lives for the sake of the children, who now repudiate everything the parents stood for? And what a mixture of feelings must the children have? Gratitude, guilt, embarrassment, even a measure of condescension?

Ethicists typically strive for some sort of universality, for moral propositions that will hold across cultures and periods of history. Thus ethicists are likely to be uncomfortable with any situation of moral change, where yesterday's vice comes to be seen as today's virtue. In this particular instance, there is the additional problem that for most Christian and Jewish ethicists there will be a natural affinity with the ethic of production and just as natural an aversion to the new ethic of consumption. While the religious origins of Weber's Protestant ethic are no longer relevant for many people who still practice it, Christian ethicists (and not only Protestant ones) will empathize with these religious roots. Put simply, asceticism is more readily legitimated religiously than hedonism.

I am a social scientist, with only an amateur interest in ethics as a systematic discipline. A few, admittedly lay, observations on the ethical problem disclosed by the preceding argument will have to suffice.

Evidently, how one approaches this problem will depend on how one understands the relation of religious faith and morality. If one believes that moral judgments can be directly derived from faith—be it via the Scriptures, or tradition, or a combination of these with the insights of natural law—then one must presumably strive to formulate an ethic of economic behavior that will span these different situations, that will be applicable to both the earlier and the later phases of modern economic development. Clearly, this will not be an easy task.

There is another possibility. Here one understands the relation between faith and morality in a much more indirect way. Faith is not so much the source of moral judgments, but rather supplies the ontological context within which morality, like all other human experiences, ultimately makes sense. The human condition in the face of the reality to which faith testifies remains constant throughout all historical changes. Faith can only relate the moral dilemmas of the moment to this ultimate reality, but it cannot dictate codes of conduct that would be applicable to all historical situations. Such an understanding of the relation between faith and morality will invite the charge of antinomianism. Even short of that, it will inevitably be frustrating to the ethicist. It can also give a sense of liberation to those caught in the vicissitudes of social change.

Chapter 3

Reforming Wisdom from the East

Dennis P. McCann

The global era now dawning is not likely to be the Christian Century that our predecessors had fervently expected. Even if Protestant Christian ethics is reinvigorated along the lines so forcefully laid out in chapter one, partisans of this new, chastened Social Gospel will find themselves confronted by the cultural consequences of a century of Great Awakenings in the religious traditions of Asia. At the turn of the nineteenth century, the confident visage with which American Protestantism faced the future was at least partly a reflection of what turned out to be the zenith of Western civilization's waning imperial hegemony. Despite the showcasing that they received at the 1893 Parliament of the World's Religions, Asian religious traditions still seemed launched on a trajectory of irreversible decline. Protestantism and Progress, as no less a thinker than Ernst Troeltsch observed, were virtually synonymous. One hundred years later, however, the 1993 Parliament fueled suspicions that, perhaps, just the opposite was the case. The traditions of South and East Asia, not to mention a resurgent Islam, now appear to be in the ascendancy, and mainline Protestants, along with other Christians of European descent, are struggling to overcome a growing sense of internal disarray and societal decentering.

The advent of a single, globally integrated, market economy provides a singularly compelling arena in which to explore the ethical consequences of this sobering fulfillment of Western dreams of religious pluralism. Troeltsch's friend and collaborator, Max Weber, established a sociological baseline for world historical claims for the moral significance of the Reformation in his pivotal essay, *The Protestant Ethic and the Spirit of Capitalism*, with the comparative studies of China, India, and ancient Judaism (a study of Islam was never completed). The hardly coincidental convergence of Asian religious revivals and the development of a global economy no longer regulated by the Bretton Woods agreements provides a context in which to reassess Weber's perspective and how it might still provide important clues to Protestantism's ethical contribution to the decentered world of the twenty-first century. Though Weber may have been wrong about any exclusive relationship between the Protestant ethic and capitalism, the ways in which Asian religious traditions have modernized themselves and the positive impact their modernization is having upon global development seem to confirm the basic soundness of his assumption that all systems of political economy are rooted in the distinct histories of various religions.

Rethinking not only Weber's methodology, but also the substantive merits of his views on the whole spectrum of today's economically active Asian traditions, is an important prolegomenon to plotting a plausible future for Christian social ethics. Contrary to Weber's expectations, the twentieth century has witnessed the striking economic success of Roman Catholics in the United States, based on the laity's creative—and largely unacknowledged—accommodation and adaptation of the Protestant ethic. Even more unexpected from a Weberian perspective has been the success of roughly comparable forms of capitalism in Japan, and now China, where broadly neo-Confucian values have proven to be anything but an obstacle to economic development, once they are stripped of their traditional feudal-imperial embodiments. Such cases suggest that once the spirit of capitalism had succeeded in institutionalizing itself, other of the world's religious traditions could adopt and adapt its institutions while developing from within their own resources an ethical profile that prepares adherents to participate in a global economy.

To be sure, modernization does not always render religious traditions more open to capitalist development; and of those that have become more open, not all have taken the path of accommodation and adaptation at the same time and in the same way. An internal comparison, for example, of the social histories of American and Polish Catholicism would suggest just how ambiguous and hesitant this process is. Nevertheless, the decentering of economic and political power that is accompanying the decline of the Western hegemony means that Christian social ethics cannot proceed as if it were the exclusive source of moral wisdom in and for a global era. Indeed, as Western nations seek to cope with the economic dislocations resulting from both immigration and the increasing share of their domestic markets now dominated by foreign multinational corporations, the renewal of Christian social ethics must include a hard look at the long-term viability of a post-Christian society, including its own capacity to articulate and promote a distinctive cultural identity that is worth preserving.

The following conjectures about Asian religious traditions and their comparative advantages in the global era may at first seem like a distraction from the serious business with which this volume is concerned. But that is not the case. As an American Catholic I fully share a concern about a genuinely ecumenical social ethic, and I applaud attempts to move the discussion on so many issues beyond the conventional polarizations of radical, (neo-)liberal and (neo-) conservative opinion. I hope to show here that Christian social ethics may learn to rediscover some of its own moral nerve and residual strengths in the face of the impressive accomplishments of its global competitors. If it is true that nowhere is economics autonomous or devoid of religious and cultural presuppositions, Christian social ethics ought not retreat from the challenges of the global marketplace.

The revival of Asian religious traditions capable of empowering ordinary people for successful economic performance should put us on notice that effective Christian witness can no longer be identified with some metaphysical decision for socialism. Real progress toward economic and social justice in the twenty-first century depends upon a constructive religious engagement with capitalism, its institutions, their histories, and the transformative praxis of business management. If Christian social ethics proves itself incapable of such constructive engagement, clearly, there are other traditions ready to fill the spiritual vacuum created by this fruitless act of self-marginalization.

The Business Ethics of Classical Hinduism

Throughout the world, the dawn of civilization is generally marked by prayer. Skeptics may dismiss the pervasiveness of religion in antiquity as so much superstition, soon to be dispelled by further advances in science and technology. A more discerning view, however, is possible: Just what do the prayers that have been preserved tell us about the everyday concerns of our ancestors? Here is an

97

ancient prayer that, I, for one, found very surprising. It is from the *Atharva Veda* (The Book of Spells and Incantations), one of the four *samhitas* (Hymnbooks) containing the most ancient strands of Hindu tradition. This hymn speaks to our purposes, for it is dedicated to "Success in Trading":

> I stir and animate the merchant Indra: may he approach and be our guide and leader.
> Chasing ill-will, wild beast, and highway robber, may he who hath the power give me riches.
> The many paths which Gods are wont to travel, the paths which go between the earth and heaven,
> May they rejoice with me in milk and fatness that I may make rich profit by my purchase.
> With fuel, Agni! and with butter, longing, mine offering I present for strength and conquest;
> With prayer, so far as I have strength adoring—this holy hymn to gain a hundred treasures.
> Pardon this stubbornness of ours, O Agni, the distant pathway which our feet have trodden.
> Propitious unto us be sale and barter, may interchange of merchandise enrich me.
> Accept, ye twain, accordant, this libation! Prosperous be our ventures and incomings.
> The wealth wherewith I carry on my traffic, seeking, ye Gods! wealth with the wealth I offer,
> May this grow more for me, not less: O Agni, through sacrifice chase those who hinder profit![1]

The hymn is as noteworthy for what it says as for what it doesn't say. Not only are Indra (the Aryan sky warrior-king, like the Greek Zeus, the guarantor of the moral order) and Agni (the god of fire, who, among other things, is active in making ritual acts of sacrifice propitious)—two of the most important deities in the Vedic pantheon—invoked in behalf of money-making; but money-making, or commercial exchange relations generally, is clearly regarded as morally legitimate and ennobling.

Noticeably absent from the hymn is any sense that business is a morally unworthy occupation. This lack of moral ambivalence ought to strike us as surprising, if we compare it with the rather different attitude projected in the classical period of Western civilization. Aristotle's *Politics*, for example, enshrines the anti-business bias of the Hellenistic aristocracy in terms of the natural law. His economics, based as it is on the *oikos* or aristocratic household, offers a theory of property, defined first in relationship to the *oikos*, and not with reference to exchange relations in the marketplace. Understood primarily as a means of maintaining the household, property or wealth thus has a fixed or natural limit. Economics, or household management, thus generally is focused on developing the skills necessary to secure and preserve the *padrone*'s rule over his slaves, women and children. Observing such natural limits, of course, precludes making one's living by commercial exchange, a natural law argument that was destined to survive the passing of the Hellenistic civilization in which it was formulated. More than the teachings of Jesus of Nazareth, and often by being joined to them, Aristotle shaped the moral skepticism about commerce that is characteristic of much philosophical and theological social ethics to this day.

Commerce in ancient India labored under no such similar prejudice, but that does not mean that the Vedas contain teachings that are a functional substitute for Weber's modernizing Protestant ethic. The texts yield a picture that is far more complex, one in which economic activity is embedded in a larger scheme of human and cosmic purposes. The ideal moral order upheld by classical Hinduism consists in a series of interrelated quaternities, the most basic of which is the four *varnas*, commmonly known as the caste system. Already in the *Rig Veda*, the earliest of the Vedic hymnbooks, there is the famous *Purusha-sukta* ("The Primeval Sacrifice") in which a sacred Person, "Thousand-headed Purusha," is ritually dismembered in order to create the cosmos. Here is part of that hymn:

> When they divided Purusha, in how many different portions did they arrange him? What became of his mouth, what of his two arms? What were his two thighs and his two feet called?
> His mouth became the brahman; his two arms were made into the rajanya; his two thighs the vaishyas; from his two feet the shudra was born
> The moon was born from the mind, from the eye the sun was born; from the mouth Indra and Agni, from the breath (prana) the wind (vayu) was born.[2]

The ideal division of labor symbolized by the four *varnas*—here designated as Brahman, Rajanya, Vaishya, and Shudra—is just as intrinsic to the cosmic order as are the passages of the sun and moon. The Brahman are the religious hierarchy, the Rajanya—usually referred to as Kshatriya—are the warrior aristocracy, and the Vaishya are the householders, those who produce wealth, *including* the merchants. The Shudra, of course, are those who do the dirty work.

Each of these ideal *varnas* has its own distinctive set of caste duties. While there are nine duties that are "eternal" and morally oblige members of "all four orders (equally)"—"the suppression of wrath, truthfulness of speech, justice, forgiveness, begetting one's children on one's own wedded wives, purity of conduct, avoidance of quarrel, simplicity, and maintenance of dependents"—the basic sense of how one fits in the cosmic order of things is tied less to this universal ethic than it is to one's distinctive caste duties. Here are those of the Vaishya. Notice how the *Mahabharata* knows no moral distinction between commerce and animal husbandry of the sort that Aristotle decreed:

> I shall now tell thee, O Yudhishthira, what the eternal duties of the Vaisya are. A Vaisya should make gifts, study the Vedas, perform sacrifices, and acquire wealth by fair means. With proper attention he should also protect and rear all (domestic) animals as a sire protecting his sons. Anything else that he will do will be regarded as improper for him. . . . I shall tell thee what the Vaishya's profession is and how he is to earn the means of his sustenance. If he keeps (for others) six kine, he may take the milk of one cow as his remuneration; and if he keeps (for others) a hundred kine, he may take a single pair as such fee. If he trades with others' wealth, he may take a seventh part of the profits (as his share). A seventh also is his share in the profits arising from the trade in horns, but he should take a sixteenth if the trade be in hooves. If he engages in cultivation with seeds supplied by others, he may take a seventh part of the yield. This should be his annual remuneration. A Vaishya should never desire that he should not tend cattle. If a Vaishya desires to tend cattle, no one else should be employed in that task.[3]

Though cattle are regarded as the primary form of wealth, and the householder's expertise in animal husbandry is understood as the primary means of creating wealth, the Vaishya's duties will inevitably lead him into the commercial activities, which are usually seen as the exclusive prerogative of his *varna* as such.

The exceptional circumstances in which members of the other high castes, Brahman and Kshatriya, are permitted to engage in commerce tend to confirm my thesis that business ethics in the Hindu tradition is role and institution specific and not, as in Weber's Protestant ethic, a reflection of universal moral imperatives. Here is a text that suggests how important the distinction of roles is, not just for understanding business ethics, but for appreciating the very nature of the ideal moral order. Keep in mind that the hierarchical ordering of the *varnas*, in the *Manu Smriti* for instance, reflects the natural ordering of the various parts of the Purusha's cosmic body:

> Among the several occupations the most commendable are, teaching the Veda for a Brahmana, protecting the people for a Kshatriya, and trade for a Vaishya.
> But a Brahmana, unable to subsist by his peculiar occupation just mentioned, may live according to the law applicable to Kshatriyas; for the latter is next to him in rank.
> If it be asked, "How shall it be, if he cannot maintain himself by either of these occupations?" the answer is, he may adopt a Vaishya's mode of life, employing himself in agriculture and rearing cattle. . . .
> But he who, through a want of means of subsistence, gives up the strictness with respect to his duties, may sell, in order to increase his wealth, the commodities sold by Vaishyas, making however the following exceptions.
> He must avoid selling condiments of all sorts, cooked food and sesamum, stones, salt, cattle, and human beings;
> All dyed cloth, as well as cloth made of hemp, or flax, or wool, even though they be not dyed, fruit, roots, and medical herbs;
> Water, weapons, poison, meat, Soma, and perfumes of all kinds, fresh milk, honey, sour milk, clarified butter, oil, wax, sugar, Kusagrass;
> All beasts of the forest, animals with fangs or tusks, birds, spirituous liquor, indigo, lac, and all one-hoofed beasts. . . .[4]

The extraordinary detail in this list of exceptions suggests two things. First, that modern India's cultural bias toward an extraordinarily complicated system of commercial regulations seems to go back a long time. Second, that the specific items in which non-Vaishyas are forbidden to trade are not prohibited because they are universally immoral as, say, we might regard trafficking in illegal drugs. Castes higher than vaishya cannot trade in these items—even if they are forced to abandon their caste duties and go into business—because illegitimate contact with them may incur a penalty for ritual impurity.

The four *varnas*, however, merely scratch the surface of Hindu business ethics. Each of the three higher castes, which alone participates fully in the religious life of classical Hinduism, exhibits an ideal pattern of occupations—the four *ashramas*—which define still further the moral order distinctive of each stage of life. The four *ashramas*—student, householder, retiree, and homeless wanderer or *sannyasin*—spell out how the various stages in life participate in the common pursuit of the four normative goals of human existence. The four goals—*dharma* (the pursuit of virtue or preservation of the moral order), *artha* (wealth), *kama* (sensual pleasure) and *moksha* (ultimate liberation)—suggest that the ultimate meaning of life consists in overcoming *samsara*, the wheel or, if you will, the treadmill of rebirths. This lofty, but bleak account describes the human predicament as a potentially infinite series of lifetimes, in which each person struggles to liberate oneself from this world, by achieving *nirvana*. *Nirvana* should not be confused with the Heaven longed for by orthodox Christians; *nirvana* is the cessation of *samsara*. It is the void in which there is no further necessity of rebirth. *Moksha*, the ultimate goal, means finally overcoming the world as we know it. The higher castes are closer to this goal; they are reborn to their higher status precisely because of the degree of success they've previously had in living the *dharmas* assigned to them.

I find this to be an astonishingly powerful religious vision. But we cannot pause here to contemplate its varied ethical implications. Since our focus is on religious resources for business ethics, we must confine ourselves to the penultimate goals, especially *artha* and *kama*, the pursuit of wealth and pleasure, and their overriding significance in the *dharma* specific to the householder stage in life. The Hindu householder, like the Hellenistic *padrone*, presides over an extended family and its dependents. No question; this is also the template of traditional patriarchy. But the patriarchal household, like it or not, was the central economic institution in this society. Upon the householder devolves the responsibilities of management, which are inevitably a mixture of religious, familial, and business duties. Social responsibility, including whatever care the destitute were likely to receive from their neighbors, was incumbent upon the householder, who possessed the means of helping others precisely because he was skilled at creating and preserving wealth.

The following text suggests the ideal of selflessness proper to the stage in life devoted to *artha* and *kama*:

A householder should perform every day a Smriti rite. . . . He should perform a Vedic rite on the sacred fires. . . .

Offering of the food oblation, offerings with the utterance *svadha*, performance of Vedic sacrifices, study of the sacred texts, and honoring of guests—these constitute the five great daily sacrifices dedicated respectively to the spirits, the manes, the gods, the Brahman, and men.

He should offer the food oblation to the spirits [by throwing it in the air] out of the remnant of the food offered to the gods. He should also cast food on the ground for dogs, untouchables, and crows.

Food, as also water, should be offered by the householder to the manes and men day after day. He should continuously carry on his study. He should never cook for himself only.

Children, married daughters living in the father's house, old relatives, pregnant women, sick persons, and girls, as also guests and servants—only after having fed these should the householder and his wife eat the food that has remained. . . .

Having risen before dawn the householder should ponder over what is good for the Self. He should not, as far as possible, neglect his duties in respect of the three ends of man, namely, virtue, material gain, and pleasure, at their proper times.

Learning, religious performances, age, family relations, and wealth—on account of these and in the order mentioned are men honored in society. By means of these, if possessed in profusion, even a shudra deserves respect in old age.[5]

Clearly, the pursuit of wealth traditionally enjoined upon the Hindu householder is anything but a pretext for possessive individualism.

I have suggested that classical Hinduism's role-specific ethics of *dharma* may be a more promising point of departure for business ethics than the classical Western heritage enshrined in the texts of Hellenistic philosophers like Aristotle. Not that Hindu *dharma* is morally superior to Greek *arete* (or virtue ethics), but that in our Western penchant for ethical universality, we—or at least, some of Aristotle's disciples, notably the influential philosopher Alasdair MacIntyre—have tended to decontextualize Aristotle's comments on money-making, as if they were meant, not as prudent advice to future *padrones*, but as an eternally valid judgment on the ethical merits of careers in business as such. Aristotle can plausibly be read either way; the Hindu tradition, however, suffers from no such equivocation. A virtuous life in business is not only not an oxymoron; it is the specific way in which Vaishyas fulfill their religious duties, and by implication, their moral duties to the rest of society, beginning with their own dependents—although we cannot ignore the structural ways in which this activity and its practitioners were subordinated to the rule of the princes and the *literati* values of the priests.

Such a perspective, thus, is still a far cry from Weber's Protestant ethic. The ultimate goal of life, seeking the *moksha* that overcomes *samsara*, clearly suggests the other-worldly asceticism that Weber regarded as a barrier to capitalist development. But the penultimate goals in life—*dharma, artha,* and *kama*—are also given their due, and in a manner that could prove to be more encouraging to business than comparable traditions in the classical antiquity of the West. Why, then, did not the spirit of capitalism first emerge in India? One could cite India's long history of colonial oppression, to be sure, beginning with the Moghul Empire and, later, the hegemony of the British East India Company, and culminating in the British Raj that reserved to itself control over modern India's economy.

Weber, however, was less impressed by the political history than by the typical patterns of Hindu social organization. He felt that modern capitalism required a degree of impersonalism in business relationships that could be sustained only on the basis of a universal ethic that, in a biblical sense, was no respecter of persons. Business was best kept separate from family affairs; favoritism based on kinship or other forms of social dependency would necessarily inhibit successful economic performance. The Protestant ethic, in his view, provided the key to capitalist development, not simply because of its fresh perspective on worldly affairs, but because it encouraged covenantal forms of association that, in principle, were open to strangers. Business enterprises could be "hived off" from the patriarchal household, and managed on the basis of impersonal, contractual agreements, a universal framework of commercial law that embodied, at least in part, the covenantal moral imperatives of Protestant Christianity.

Weber, therefore, remained pessimistic about the future of modern capitalism in Asia, because he could find nothing in the traditional cultures of India and China equivalent to the Protestant ethic. Nevertheless, modern capitalism, as we have seen, has found a home in Asia, and Asia has become successful enough to be globally competitive, not just as a major exporter of manufactured goods, but as an alternative model to our customary thinking about economics and business management. What Weber regarded as most likely to retard capitalist development in Asia, namely, the various cultures' primary commitment to business organization based on kinship and other forms of social dependency, now strikes many observers as the secret to Asian economic success. We turn, then, to east Asia, where the religious significance of kinship is as well documented as the successful economic performance of its corporations. Is there a connection between the two?

Capitalism and East Asian Family Values

East Asia's extraordinary record of economic growth is not news, and hasn't been news for the past quarter of a century. What such growth means for the global economy, and how it is reshaping the prospects for U.S. economic development, however, are important strategic questions whose answers will determine, as they are already determining, the challenges as well as the opportunities in which Christian social ethics must define its own future. My immediate concern, however, is with the religious dimensions of the East Asian challenge. To what extent is East Asia's success based on cultural factors that, inevitably, are religiously rooted? How do religious values continue to shape the meaning of economic activity in this region and the forms of business organization in which it is carried out?

Empirical inquiry into the nature of an "East Asian Development Model" tend to presuppose the so-called post-Confucian hypothesis. This theory explores a possible link between the powerful and pervasive influence of Confucianism upon what has been characterized as East Asia's Sinitic civilization and the region's distinctive patterns of modernization and economic development. The Confucian influence is particularly apparent in Japan and the newly industrializing countries, heretofore restricted to the "four little tigers," South Korea, Taiwan, Hong Kong, and Singapore, but now also including much of coastal China, Vietnam, Malaysia, Indonesia, and Thailand. The hypothesis asserts that a modernized form of Confucianism—what Robert M. Bellah aptly called "bourgeois Confucianism"[6]—is as important for understanding the distinctive success of the East Asian development model as is the recent political and economic history of the region. If the hypothesis is confirmed, it will tend to reinforce the argument that we've made so far regarding Weber's views of capitalism and religious values, but it will also show how modernizing inherited religious traditions, rather than aban-

105

doning them entirely, can actually work to enhance a nation's prospects for economic development.

There are few direct affinities linking classical Hinduism with Confucianism, but both religious perspectives tend to legitimate the household as the central economic and social unit in society. The bedrock of Chinese cultural tradition is emphatically this-worldly, and apparently knows nothing of the other-worldly concerns governing classical Hinduism's pursuit of *moksha*. Sacred powers, gods and goddesses, including the living spirits of dead ancestors, exert a powerful influence upon this world. They are as real, and just as unpredictable, as we are. Religious practice therefore seeks to establish a mutually beneficial accommodation between the sacred and the profane, a harmonious balance of power that is thought to reflect the will of Heaven (*T'ien*), the ultimate—though hardly personal—embodiment of the cosmic order itself (*Tao*).

The moral emphasis in Confucianism is unmistakable. The core of ethical concern is expressed in the concept of *hsiao* or filiality, which is the ideal governing the nucleus of social relationships in the Chinese household. *Hsiao* is to be realized in all five of these relationships: children to their parents; subjects to their ruler; wife to husband; younger brother to older brother; younger friend to older friend. Each of these, obviously, is hierarchical, involving a subordinate and a superior; yet each also involves mutual obligations and mutual respect. Indeed, the whole of social ethics can be understood as a "rectification of names," insofar as each of these relationships carries its own objective standards. To achieve right relationship one must recognize what is at stake in the name given it. The *hsiao* that a subject owes his ruler, for example, is implicit in what it means to be subject and what it means to be ruler.

Asian family values, as commonly discussed in analyses of East Asia's strategic strengths in the global economy, are the pervasive and enduring heritage of the Confucian ethic of *hsiao*. To be sure, modern Japanese business corporations are not simply an extension of the premodern Sinitic household. But the link between the two has been documented in various studies, and that link is highly suggestive of the ways in which modernizing religious traditions are economically significant. One such study is Koichi Shinohara's "Religion and Economic Development in Japan: An Exploration Focusing on the Institution of Ie."[7] *Ie*, like its Chinese cognate *jia*, refers to house or household, in a sense roughly equivalent to the classical Greek *oikos*, the Latin *domus*, and the Spanish *casa*. As Shinohara asserts, "*Ie* is best understood as the basic unit of communal life and consists of all those who live under one roof and eat meals prepared in the same kitchen." He uses here a broad definition, in order not to restrict the *ie* to blood kinship as such. Adoptions are common within the traditional *ie*. In order to preserve continuity within the household, it is customary for widows to remain within their former husbands' *ie* in order to raise the children there. Typically, the *ie* is internally differentiated, as subordinate branches of the family (*bunke*) can be established in relation to the main branch (*honke*), whose head (*kacho*) retains substantial control of all household property.

How the religious and moral values embedded in the premodern *ie* came to dominate modern Japanese business practices can be explained as a process of cultural diffusion. Shinohara argues that the internal differentiation of *honke* and *bunke* within the *ie*, and its distinctive approach to household property, provided the model for the prewar Japanese enterprise groups known as *zaibatsu*. The *ie* structure, in other words, always was an economic unit; the major change was from a village-oriented agricultural system to an urban industrial economy. As the power of the traditional households declined, Japanese industries increasingly took up, first, the social functions of the *ie*, and later, its distinctive pattern of religious and moral values. It is little wonder, then, as Hamabata has shown in another highly pertinent study,[8] that in many Japanese firms there is an extraordinary degree of continuity linking religious, familial, and business concerns. Religious rites are exercised and social responsibilities are discharged, quite naturally, within the firm itself, to a degree that defies modern Western assumptions about the boundaries separating the sacred from the secular. Policies considered typical of Japanese corporations, e.g., lifetime employment, wage distribution based on seniority, management by consensus, and an egalitarian atmosphere within the firm, are shown by Shinohara to be expressions of the enduring influence of the *ie* as a template for Japanese social organization.

Shinohara helpfully concludes his analysis with a parting shot at Max Weber. From a Weberian perspective, because the modern Japanese corporation reflects the social logic of the traditional *ie*, it ought not to succeed—at least, not when measured against any rigorous standard of economic performance. It lacks the impersonalism characteristic of a company of strangers whose relationships are primarily contractual; it will be debilitated by nepotism, Weber would have predicted, and will typically pursue policies that are economically irrational. Japan's impressive economic success may, however, suggest—as it does to James Fallows—that our own assumptions about what is and is not economically rational are arbitrary, and if not irrational as such, at least as derivative from inherited religious and moral norms as any alternative system.[9] Fallows makes a distinction between an autonomous and a "culturally embedded" economy, which within the limits of neo-classical theory is a contradiction in terms. Japan's economy is culturally embedded in the sense that it is organized to fulfill certain "noneconomic" purposes, the chief of which is national security, broadly understood. Its corporations, as we have seen, are not only a reflection of Asian family values, but an effective instrument for preserving them. This system may be economically irrational; but it seems to perform well in the global economy.

Shinohara's essay responds most effectively to Weber's fears about nepotism. He shows that, even in its premodern reality, the *ie* was geared to successful economic performance. The custom of adoption, as discussed above, allowed the *kacho* to designate an heir, either when he lacked a son of his own, or when his heir had already shown signs of being grossly incompetent. The household's collective future, including its accumulated property, was not to be frittered away by someone who showed no inclination to live by the ethic of *hsiao*—known in Japanese as *ko*. As Shinohara comments, managing the affairs of the *ie* involved "a significant level of economic rationalism." Though the social responsibilities of kinship were exercised through the *ie*, family ties were not allowed to threaten the *ie's* own survival. Such an approach to economic performance is clearly seen in Japanese firms, where a manager is not likely to be fired for his failures, but he is also not likely to be given anything else of much importance to do. Clearly, there are ways to keep most people productive, even in a system guaranteeing lifetime employment. Tenured professors and functionally tenured clergy should have little difficulty imagining how this is done!

Rethinking Corporate Social Responsibility

This brief foray into the field of comparative religious ethics may suggest fresh resources for understanding the nature of corporate social responsibility. If the history of American business were all we had to go on, the movement for corporate responsibility could be regarded as an external impetus stemming largely from religious communities animated by the Protestant Social Gospel, or its analogues in other, mostly Christian traditions. Religious activists, in such a scenario, seek to humanize the modern business corporation by imposing values known from other sources, and honored in other (not-for-profit) forms of social organization. Christian social ethics in a global era, however, should not perpetuate this all-too-common misunderstanding of the nature and task of corporate social responsibility. For on such an assumption, neither the agenda for corporate social responsibility already implicit in sound business practice, nor its theoretical basis in the Reformation's own views of covenantal association can be fully appreciated.

The distinctive contribution of Christian social ethics to any future discussion of corporate social responsibility ought to rest on this covenantal understanding. Holding the modern business corporation socially accountable is not, therefore, an imposition of an ethical agenda extraneous to sound business practice, but is already operative—though usually only implicit—in what it means for any given firm to be, and to seek to remain, in business. This is a difficult claim to make, only if we allow ourselves to be mesmerized by current legal definitions of managerial responsibility. Precisely here, the evidence available from the comparative study of religious social ethics can be an eye-opener. Our Asian competitors make no bones about the ultimately religious logic of their own forms of business organization, and its influence upon their ways of defining what can and cannot be demanded by way of corporate social responsibility. Learning from their experience might lead us to recognize analogous resources in our own situation, long repressed by presumptions about the inevitable secularization of the world, the purely secular character of economic life, and the immorality of commercial life derived from Hellenistic ethics.

The challenge afforded by Asian development in a global era might not only lead us to rediscover the cultural embeddedness of our own ways of thinking about economics and business, but to recover and recast the enduring roots of our thinking from Western religious traditions, even in view of their historic vicissitudes. It might even inspire us to cultivate anew our civilization's authentically Christian roots, so that we might learn once again what we mean to each other, and what we owe each other, as members of a company of strangers. Whether we like it or not, the original template for Western business corporations remains biblical and covenantal. We can renew Christian social ethics for the twenty-first century only if we learn once again how to nurture, reform, and deploy that template effectively.

Chapter 4

God's *Oikonomia* and the New World Economy

M. Douglas Meeks

Despite some impressive exceptions, it has been difficult for modern Christian theology and ethics to relate to economics. The reasons are clear: it has been considered against the scientific and cultural rules to invade the autonomous territory of the science of economics, governed as it is by its own internal laws. Furthermore, modern liberal theology has assumed that it has to accede to the agenda given it by enlightened boundaries of knowledge and judgment. For at least two centuries it has been considered logically impossible, unwise, or even dangerous to think of God and economy together.

What separates modern economics from traditional economics, so that it is assumed that modern economics is in fact an entirely new science, is that God is presumed absent from the market.[1] In their modern cast, theology and church are not supposed to be responsible for questions of public life. Theology and church have more and more confined themselves to the realms of meaning and purpose for the internal life, to the sphere of the private. Often the church's economic dealings are restricted to the narrowest conception of stewardship as institutional maintenance. How to put economy and theology together in any significant sense seems to be a major conundrum. Does the church's teaching about God and its life in God make any difference for its teaching about economy and its mission in what Daniel Bell has called the "public household"?

Despite its stupendous accomplishments in other respects, the central difficulty with modern economics, as Karl Polanyi has argued, is that it has omitted what was the primary concern of traditional economy, namely, *livelihood*. No one can doubt the great gains in economy due to the creation of the modern science of economics. The astounding rise in productivity and in the living standards of millions of people seem to justify the official absence of God and human livelihood in the theory and practice of the market. The promises of the market are so great that for many people its language, concepts, and mechanisms represent the most universal reality. And, yet, despite the great gains of the science of economics, millions around the world feel powerless economically and resigned to poverty as though it were destiny.

If, however, we acknowledge the most ancient question of *oikonomia* (*oikos* + *nomos*)—"Will everyone in the household get what it takes to live?"—then it will be no surprise that up to the Enlightenment, economy was at the heart of Christian theology and ethics. Economy was understood in such a broad sense that the "economic" Trinity described the creating, redeeming, and new-creating work of God in the whole of creation, and economy in human terms referred broadly to the relationships of those within a household toward their survival (*servivre* = "living through") and the life of their environment against the powers of death. A Christian theology that wants to stay faithful to the biblical narratives cannot give up these senses of "economy" and therefore will engage modern economics especially at the point at which it disregards human and natural livelihood. There is, to be sure, not one single technical economic problem of our time that can be solved by reference to Scripture. But the uncovering of God's trinitarian history with the world as seen in the biblical narratives also uncovers a way of being in the world out of which the church can make its contribution to reshaping the "public household."

The Trinitarian Oikonomia

A Christian ethics of economy finds its locus in God's *oikonomia*, that is, God's all-inclusive trinitarian history with the creation. All things are created by God for God's ultimate reign in righteousness and glory. This means that all ethical questions have an eschatological horizon. All questions of economy are judged according to this eschatological reality which in the life, death, and resurrection of Jesus Christ has already dawned in this world of death and destruction. Biblical apocalyptic is transmuted into eschatology. God gives God's own life for the sake of the world and is already coming to dwell in it as God prepares the world to be God's own home. Because God loves the world with God's own life and gives Godself for the sake of its life (John 3:16; Rom. 8:32), the Christian congregation has to eschew all dualisms that denigrate the body and nature. The whole creation is aimed teleologically toward God's sabbath in which every creature will be reconciled, justified, and glorified and thus embodied in God's eternal life. This can already be experienced in the sacrament of Communion.

This view of the cosmic reign of Christ and the universal indwelling of God's Holy Spirit in all things is centered on God's power of suffering love in and through which God creates, redeems, and renews the world. The power of God's suffering which comes to expression in the "weakness" and "folly" of the cross (1 Cor. 1), is the only power that is stronger than death and that will not destroy itself. It is this love alone that can mediate God's righteousness and justice to the world; it is this love alone that enables human beings to practice God's justice. This love is God's nature and because God cannot deny Godself, it is the essence of the covenant by which God is *for* God's creation, not by sovereign whim or pure choice but rather by God's *being as love*. This covenant is the character of creation. The good news of the gospel is that the reign of God is actually beginning under the conditions of history, that is, in the midst of sin, evil, and death. Thus a Christian ethic of economy will be thoroughly sacramental in character. It sees the infinite in the finite, the eternal in time, and God's justice in the negation of injustice. This approach to Christian ethics will emphasize the rights of nature and human embodiment over against the modern trends toward abstract power over nature and the body.

Christian ethics will in the end perceive freedom, love, and justice out of the life and work of God. The Cappadocian Fathers offered the most helpful insight into God's immanent life as seen in the biblical narratives with their notion of *perichoresis*. According to this teaching, the divine persons are who they are in relationship to the others, and yet they remain distinct persons. This view of trinitarian relations provides a paradigm by which to understand individuality and community. The reality of community makes possible the distinctiveness of persons, and the distinctiveness of persons makes possible the reality of community. Christian ethics thus finds its criterion of personhood and community in the love that binds by making every individual free and frees through the power of self-giving. It will, for example, decide against both "progressive individualism" and "collectivity" as determinative modalities of human existence. And because it is only this love and this freedom that can mediate life-giving and creative justice, the Christian view of justice will stand over against any sense of justice that negates this love and this freedom.

A primary difficulty facing a Christian ethics of economy, however, is that though the church is under messianic orders to be the household of Jesus Christ, it is itself so absorbed by the market logic that it has little new to offer the great debates about the future of economy. Thus, to make a genuine contribution to alternative economy in the world, the church itself would have to be radically restructured and "recultured" by its own gospel.

Therefore, Christian theological and ethical work on economy must be *ecclesiological*; that is, it has to be concerned with how the church can become free enough from the market society actually to live the alternative *oikonomia tou theou* (economy of God) out of which it can gain its solidarity with the world and its critical and constructive contribution to economy. It may well be that the future of the world depends on whether it can become something like one household in which radically different people and peoples can live for each other's lives and for the life of nature. But to serve this purpose, the church would have radically to rethink God and economy in the context of a general understanding of the common life—God's and ours.

Economy, Politics, and Community

An expansive dream that has persisted at least since the onset of neo-classical economics is that economy can and should function without politics and without community.[2] But the result of separating economy from community and politics is a set of economistic laws that make decisions for us. The market is an organizing (and conveniently invisible) mechanism, like that which the deistic God of earlier centuries set in motion—that is, automatic. It allows us to avoid public encounter and decision-making and trades citizenship in a polis for consumerism in a market. But, in point of fact, economy can be transformed only through politics and community, and indeed even market economy depends on some configuration of community and politics, even if they are covert in its theory.

114

For the foreseeable future all public economy will be market oriented. But the rules of the market are human constructions and can be reshaped in order to make the market more humane—through politics and community. At the same time, politics and community face the problem that no political means exist for humanizing the economy without communities to bear them, and the market economy, as interpreted by economic theory, tends to destroy community.

The difficulty of juxtaposing theology and economy is this: The absolute prevailing logic of our society is the market logic. Robert Heilbroner claims that the nature of our society is *accumulation of wealth as power* and that the logic of our society is *exchange of commodities*.[3] Everything dances around these realities. We believe them so implicitly that we are willing to serve them and shape our lives according to their logic. It is the language with which all people are fascinated. It is increasingly the logic through which people the world over expect life, security, and future.

The market logic is in and of itself a human good. It is perhaps the most successful human social device ever conceived. No one can deny its awesome effect in modernity. But we do need radically to criticize many of the so-called neo-classical assumptions of the modern market. These assumptions destroy the possibility of Christian discipleship within economy and are increasingly narrowing the public space of appearance in which the church can exist. They destroy the possibility of democracy shaping property, work, and consumption in ways that preserve equality, participation, and access to livelihood and community. The market can flourish without these assumptions and many of the institutions to which they have given rise. It is not the market per se but rather what Karl Polanyi calls "the market society" that should be opposed.[4] This would mean criticizing a society in which all the spheres in which social goods have to be distributed are controlled by the market logic itself. All social goods are produced and distributed as if they were commodities. This means the decisive question about economy today is a cultural question.

If the Household of Jesus Christ has a memory, we know that there are certain social goods that should be distributed according to a different logic because these social goods are themselves not commodities. Food, healing, learning, the generation of the generations, belonging, justice, and respect should not be commodities or exhaustively commodities. The market is the greatest mechanism we have ever devised for producing and distributing commodities. But if something is not a commodity, should it be distributed according to the market logic or is there another logic for the distribution of those things necessary for life and life abundant? What is necessary for life cannot be a commodity or exclusively a commodity. In the market society, however, there is nothing that cannot, in principle, be distributed as a commodity.

The New World Economy

Few contemporary economists doubt that we are undergoing a worldwide structural transformation of economy. The *industrial age* is giving way to the *information age*. Massive reorganization of business and government combined with the unprecedented influence of high technology, global financial systems, and the power of electronic media have led to what is being referred to as "the end of organized capitalism" that can no longer be thought of in terms of the "wealth of nations."[5]

The process of globalization is accompanied by utopian and dystopian predictions. The end of the Cold War brought the lifting of enormous financial, social, and psychological burdens and the expectation of unprecedented opportunity symbolized by the computer chip and fiber optics. But the dystopic perspective sees the possibility of cataclysmic collapse due to the debt crisis, the poverty crisis, and the ecological/energy crisis, and the increase of wild, ungovernable zones in the world and its cities. The disorganization of capitalism does not mean in any sense the end of the market but rather the disintegration of many of the social, economic, political, and cultural structures that attended the capitalist societies of the nineteenth and twentieth centuries. A core assumption remains, namely, that our individual material futures, pursued according to the rules of the market and directed by the invisible hand of technology, will result in a beneficent common future for all. In this sense we may still speak of a market society in the midst of disorganized capitalism.

Mobility and Whirl

There have been immensely powerful transformations of mobility in disorganized capitalism. Personal mobility of business agents, tourists, migrants, and refugees has increased enormously. There has been a time-space compression in financial markets that makes market transactions almost instantaneous. This has produced a generalization of risks that knows no national boundaries and of the fear of such risks. Major parts of the world economy are now international producer and consumer *services*. Globalized culture and communication structures become increasingly free of particular regions and locate in global cities more closely connected to each other than to their provinces. In these cities a service and information class develops with cosmopolitan taste, especially for fashionable consumer services, usually provided by one or another category of immigrant. Social classes, conventionally organized around symbolic place and hierarchy, give way to a new kind of cosmopolitan postmodern individualism in re-engineered cultural spaces (e.g., the art world, the financial world, the drug world, the advertising world, the academic world). And, perhaps most important, the disorganization of capitalist society is marked by the declining effectiveness and legitimacy of nation-states which are unable to control such disorganized capitalist flows; government can no longer control economy.

Wealth and Work

In the midst of the disorganization of capitalism it is increasingly difficult to speak of "national" economies. Few American firms or industries compete against foreign firms or industries. Much more typical now is the "global web," as described by Robert Reich:

> . . . perhaps headquartered in and receiving much of its financial capital from the United States, but with research, design, and production facilities spread over Japan, Europe, and North America; additional production facilities in Southeast Asia and Latin America; marketing and distribution centers on every continent; and lenders and investors in Taiwan, Japan, and West Germany as well as the United States. This ecumenical company competes with similarly ecumenical companies headquartered in other nations. Battle lines no longer correspond with national borders.[6]

In this global economy the economic well-being of persons in a nation depends on the value they add to the global economy through their work, skills, information control, and insights.

In the global economy the interlocking character of what Reich calls the "symbolic analysts" worldwide is accompanied by their decreasing dependence on other economic actors in their own country and region. The income of symbolic analysts has increased dramatically in the last fifteen years while the income of routine producers and in-person servers has dramatically declined. Decline in their income has meant less access to good education, health care, job training for the latter two classes and thus increasing exclusion from what it takes to become a symbolic analyst.

The burden of poverty has always fallen disproportionately on a few groups, such as people of color, children, and women heads of households. African American and Hispanic families are nearly three times more likely to be poor than white families. The rate of poverty is even higher among Native Americans. One-fifth of all children in this country live in poor households. But in the global economy we have also an increasing segregation by income. The number of working poor is growing everywhere. The national household and the global household are dividing up in ways that make it impossible to give all people access to what it takes to live and live abundantly.

Poverty and Wealth

Perhaps most frightening in the global household is the way in which those with economic power are dropping out of the community. They are removing themselves and their wealth from the commonweal, which is the precondition for the political transformation of economy toward justice. Symbolic analysts "are quietly seceding from larger and diverse publics of America into homogeneous enclaves, within which their earnings need not be redistributed to people less fortunate than themselves."[7] This leads to two separate cities, two residential patterns, two school systems, two systems of health care delivery, and two systems of welfare and security.

On the global scene the three major economic blocs in the First World—the European Community, North America (with Mexico in tow), and Japan (closely associated with South Korea, Taiwan, Singapore and,until 1997, Hong Kong)—are withdrawing from a household whose rules would assure the inclusion of the world's poor. "This foreshadows the development of a two track world economy, with these three regions in a fast track and most others in a slow one which will fall further and further behind, to the point of being effectively excluded from the dominant economic systems."[8]

The clearest index of poverty is hunger. Although the world food supply can provide enough for all, some seven hundred million people do not get sufficient food for an active and healthy life. In its first five years of life one out of every three children is undernourished. Forty-two thousand children die of starvation every day. Persistent hunger throughout the world dooms new generations of children to the lifelong problems caused by severe malnutrition at an early age. Nearly two thousand million lack potable water. Nine hundred million cannot read or write.

The only thing that seems to be keeping people alive in the degrading conditions of shantytowns around the world is something like a community, a household. Where it comes from is hard to say. These people live outside and against the formal economy. They can expect nothing from it. They expect nothing from the state. But somehow there are household rules and resources for life that are keeping them alive. We have to ask ourselves whether simply extending the market logic as we know it will save these people, or whether extending the market logic into these settings would destroy the very community that is keeping the people alive. It gives one an awesome sense of despair in the face of a possible unimaginable destruction of human life.

These conditions create a cauldron of resentment in barrios and ghettos and are leading in the last decade of the twentieth century to new levels of dislocation, immigration, and homelessness in many parts of the world. In the United States, ownership of land by working farm families and rural community life are deeply threatened. The flight of capital and factory closings have left whole communities without a means of livelihood. Northern countries try to make a distinction between political and economic immigration but generally welcome the more talented persons as well as workers willing to accept wages much lower than the standard in the host country.

The dystopic view of the disorganization of capitalist society includes the increase of "wild zones" or "ungovernable spaces" in the impacted ghettos of First World inner cities, in wide expanses of Eastern Europe, and in the Third World. These are areas of thorough deindustrialization in which almost all institutions of civil society have collapsed or exited: health and welfare organizations, churches, schools, neighborhood associations, trade unions, and the like.[9] William Julius Wilson describes the underclass in impacted American ghettos in terms of these characteristics: living in a space isolated from other social classes; long-term unemployment; female-headed households; lack of training and skills; long periods of poverty and welfare dependency; and a tendency to be absorbed in street crime.[10] Wilson points to the insidious presence of structural racism in that African Americans as individuals were following the rules to take their place in American society when the very structures for which they were aspiring were moved. A horror in the present global household is that we are getting used to the desolation of these wild zones and seem to be "writing off" whole sectors and generations of people as if they did not belong to the human household.

A Participatory Civic Democracy

The period of the "disorganization of capitalism" is also a period of the weakening of democracy. A growing fear of the future produces political discourse that obscures rather than illuminates, separates rather than associates. The mass media's reflection of so-called public opinion eclipses public virtue. People have no public space in which they can reflect on the close ties between their personal and public lives. Public institutions are adrift and almost none supports a disciplined public conversation on how we can achieve a socially just, economically equitable, and environmentally sustainable future. Without hope for the future the energy necessary for democracy is depleted.

Democracy works by bringing the power of self-interest and collective interest into accountability to the public good. The crisis of democracy is its weakness in representing the rights of the poor, the young, the aged, the coming generations, and nature. If we mean by democracy the systematic criticism of privilege so that all may have an equal opportunity of participation in decisions about their living and the fulfillment of their lives, then we are speaking of an instrument that has a rough analogy to God's Torah and Gospel concern to create economy that serves communities of life against death. One of the strongest institutions assuring the continuation of the present practice of the market is free trade. But it is increasingly threatening the very being of democracy.[11]

What would be an alternative to the control of the world economy by multinational corporations and a global political authority unresponsive to the poor and ordinary citizens? An alternative vision may require questioning the largely unexamined assumptions of free trade.[12] Is it true that the greater the increase of gross national product (GNP), the better? The increase of the GNP in expanded markets can be connected with the increase of the wealth of the rich but not with improvement of the welfare of the poor. The market does not measure the price of Third World people taking on the market culture and modes of behavior overnight, as it were, when in point of fact it took First World people decades, if not centuries, to become adept. The growth of the GNP does not necessarily measure improvement of human welfare. Alternative indices of economic welfare have shown that welfare has not grown proportionately to per capita GNP in recent decades. If economic welfare in the broadest sense, rather than increase in the GNP, is the ethical goal, then there is no ethical compulsion to increase the size of markets. In fact, ethical considerations count strongly against it.

An alternative to free trade could be a system of relatively self-sufficient markets in relatively small regions. In each of these regions the community can organize through political and social institutions to make certain that its members are included in the household. A market economy without bureaucratic planning can accompany the community's establishing of rules, applied equally to all members of the public household, designed to support the public good in health, environmental well-being, and the conditions of labor and to assure that its members have access to what it takes to live and live with human fulfillment. Contemporary forms of communal autarchy would have to assure that those who played by these rules would not be forced to compete with other producers who played by less demanding rules in other markets. The market, for example, would have to be complex enough to ensure competition in as many sectors as possible. What Martin Buber called "communities of communities" would, of course, require considerable power to enforce such rules. But the power should emerge from the communities themselves. First steps in this direction have to be taken through the emerging global civil society which works toward distributed power and knowledge.

If our best chance for a global household of justice is the democratization of economy, this would require radical changes in the way we form, accumulate, and distribute capital; in our understanding of property, work, and consumption; and in our tax, insurance, welfare, and security systems. These changes can only be made politically. But where are the communities that could envision and bear such a politics? The church is not itself meant to be such a political community, but it is meant to be a community that makes such communities possible.

The Roots of Community

We have seen that the church has been to a large extent absorbed into the market society and is itself in significant ways organized according to the market logic. Can we speak concretely of the presence of God in the Spirit making room and time for the embodiment of the church so that it can actually appear publicly and make an historical difference? How does the church block the spread of the totalitarian tendencies of the market so that, dwelling in God, it can be an alternative *oikonomia*?

Unless we are focused on ecclesial community, we have little actual means to address in any significant public way the transformation of the economic and political subjugating realities that are causing massive human misery in the global community. We have been too much caught up in the Enlightenment sciences of the individual and of the social subject to the virtual exclusion of the interhuman, mutually indwelling community, which is the primary mode of *ecclesia*.

Without what Immanuel Levinas calls "the community of face," the radical criticism and alternative community necessary to freedom from subjugation will not take place.[13] Here Edward Farley's distinction of three spheres of human reality is helpful: (1) the sphere of subjectivity or the agent, (2) the social sphere, and (3) the sphere of reciprocal human relation.[14] In their increasing dependence on the psychological and sociological sciences, theology and ethics have lost sight of the fact that both evil and redemption have a primary locus in the community of the face, that is the sphere of household relationships in which human beings mutually coinhere.

Those in the liberal tradition have a predilection for large claims for the possible transformations of individual persons and of society, transformation toward wholeness in individuals and justice in society, without paying attention to what could be the actual historical bearers of such transformations. The result is ecclesiastical institutions that have less and less influence publicly. Much theological discourse, therefore, cannot surmount the pervasive fatalism about changing massive institutions which has a stranglehold on our society, given the unaccountability of the market to democratic process and the seeming impossibility of democratically structured change. Recently it has become commonplace to ask whether there are any communities that can nourish democratic values or that can bear politics. Our question is to what extent there can be any genuine communities of transformation in the church.

In the sphere of individual selves evil thrives in alienation, resentment, guilt, and violation stemming from idolatry. In the social sphere evil occurs when a group's self-absolutizing of its particularity violently utilizes other groups. The peculiar power of evil is that it separates the spheres of the self and of the social from the human mutual indwelling, thus rendering redemption in any sphere impossible. Market relations, once they determine all relations, separate communities of face from selves and social entities, agencies and strategies, and become seemingly benign masks of subjugation. Because idolatry and self-absolutizing can be overcome only in the intersubjective, redemption takes place in the sphere of the mutual coinherence of human beings with each other and with nature. If culturally mediated norms for regulating human action as sedimented in the market culture can be criticized and changed only in the sphere of the interhuman, then we should search for new social forms in the depth of the community of face.

There are many distinctive disciplines of the church's practice under its own criteria of face which must be retrieved and reimagined. Here I will refer to the ecclesial community of face formed at the Lord's Table as a primary locus of the alternative economy of the household of Jesus Christ.

God's Oikonomia and the Eucharist

Ecclesia is a community of face in which the sin and fear of human beings and the power of evil and death are taken into the life of God's love and the power of God's love is given to the community. This love creates an oikonomia whose habitus and background practices are epitomized in the Lord's meal. The shaping power of the household is to be seen in the table ethos. The eucharistic economy of God expresses itself in patent, objective table manners which create the ethos and ethics of the economy of the Triune God (under the conditions of history) within the community of face.

Table manners are as old as human society. They assure *sharing* and prevent *violence*. The strange table manners at the Lord's Table, however, are practices of the *oikonomia tou theou* and thus intend more than prevention of violence and sharing of what is necessary for life. They embody the *oikic perichoretic* (mutually indwelling) relationships which actually constitute life against death, evil, and sin. They are expressions of the interdivine, interhuman relations created by the Word (*logos*/logic) of the gospel in the power of the Holy Spirit.

At the Lord's Supper we have the same questions of manners and rituals that any meal has: Who is the host? Who is invited? How are hosts and guests greeted? What should be served? How should we serve it? What is the seating arrangement or how should the weakest be assured of their portion? When should we start eating? What should we talk about? How should we thank the host? How should we depart? What provision for the next meal should be made? These of course are the primary questions of economy, notwithstanding their eclipse in modern economics, that is, the primary questions of relations of the household toward life against death. The way in which these questions are answered in practice in the community of face determine the possibility and shape of the church's witness in economy. What follows can only be suggestive of this claim.

Memory, Hope, and the Host

The *oikic perichoretic* relationships of a church open to the world depend on the real presence of the Host, Jesus Christ, to create the community of face in which idolatry and subjugation can be overcome. The real presence of Jesus Christ means the mediation of the past of Jesus (including Israel and creation) and the future of Jesus (including the reign of the Triune Community's righteousness over death, evil, and sin). The market society/culture eclipses memory and hope. Without those household functions which stimulate memory and hope, there is no possibility of *oikic* community of face which grounds the possibility of criticism and innovation. Much of what is currently passing for "world openness" in terms of deconstruction of tradition is itself undermining the possibility of new *oikic* communities of face.

A Table for the Stranger

The economy of grace depends on who is invited to dinner. If we do not eat with the stranger, we will never be able to establish *oikic* relationships with the poor in any conceivable way that approximates the intention of the Triune Community's righteousness/justice.

Conventional moral norms sedimented in North American culture are thoroughly egoistic. In such a privatistic culture all public responsibility has to be defended in terms of self-interest in some kind of social contract. The church is merely a voluntary association of like-minded people who help each other with individual choices. World openness in this context can also be conceived in terms of egoism: The other completes me, helps me to come to my own self-understanding, makes me more human. The market culture retrieves with ardor every ethical argument for egoism; we are profoundly predisposed to understand rights in terms of prudence.

Only the encounter of the stranger can break self-absolutism. The encounter of the stranger at the Lord's Table is the beginning of life, the possibility of justification before God, the stuff of redemption.[15] A face is the expression of the way another person is in the world, of his or her way of experiencing the world. The face of a stranger shocks us, but it is our one chance of becoming truly human. Our salvation is wrapped up in the face of the stranger. We don't discover ourselves and our salvation by self-discovery, by looking deeper into ourselves, but in encountering the face of the other. That is the beginning of life; it is the other's appeal that gives me the opportunity to be free and just.

The Economy of Gift

Like the rest of culture in the North Atlantic rim, the church is impacted by the numbing effect of the experience of artificial scarcity and satiation. The deepest and most necessary assumption for the practice of the market logic is scarcity. The effect of the practice of the market logic is satiation. Both scarcity and satiation deaden the spirit and impede life with the other. Artificial scarcity spawns the lottery culture: the others may not make it, but I may. Satiation slakes the thirst for righteousness. Scarcity and satiation leave only one possibility for the distribution of what is necessary for life and life abundant: the logic of exchange. The genuinely other cannot appear in this logic. *Oikic* relationships become genuinely humanizing through the encounter with the other.

Eucharistic *oikic* relationships begin with forgiveness and thereby create a new economy and a new logic of distribution called grace. What is served at this meal is the gift of God's own life, the body and blood of Jesus Christ, which above all is the gift of God's forgiveness as the sole power which can break the bonds of sin, evil, and death.

Those who are forgiven are capable of extraordinary love (Luke 7:36-50). Those who are forgiven little, love little. They hoard, for they have constantly to justify themselves and construct their own immortality. If we are forgiven and loved so much that God gives God's own life for us, then much is expected of us. And so we leave this meal, not just having shared with each other and having prevented violence, but we leave as new creatures empowered to live with the other.

The eucharistic modality is joy so great that it judges and transforms, a judgment that is so absolute that we cannot help but be thankful that it is gift. Joy and judgment make us outraged by poverty because of the endless generosity of God and shock us with the recognition that not being in the mode of gifting and being gifted is blasphemous. The *oikonomia tou theou* depends upon the retaught and relearned generosity of God, upon gifts that give in being given and that create dignity in being received. Only the gratuitous language of praise can break the suspicion and hatred of gifting and being gifted in our public household. No one in our public household wants to be "much obliged," for it would mean by definition the loss of freedom for exchange. But unless we will mean by *oikic* relationships only what the market intends, the miracle by which we understand ourselves and our community as a gift to be gifted would have to take place:

> And God is able to provide you with every blessing in abundance, so that you may always have enough of everything and provide in abundance for every good work. As it is written,
> "He scatters abroad, he gives to the poor;
> his righteousness endures forever." (2 Cor. 9:8-9)

Conclusion

Joining the Discussion

Max L. Stackhouse

In this volume we begin a forum intended to help Christian leaders—pastors, teachers, seminarians, social activists, and business leaders—reconsider the challenges of economic life and approach a new century. It is a forum born of many dialogues in various times and places, one in which the contributors, each working from a vantage point that combines religious ethics and social analysis, show how the world of contemporary economic life and its prospects looks through a distinctive lens. The dialogue is less a series of direct responses to or criticisms of the contributions of one another than a series of perspectival "takes" on our situation that flesh out, broaden, deepen, supplement, and thereby potentially correct one another's views.

The contributors have not said all that they believe on economic matters in these essays, and each has written extensively on the issues elsewhere. Further, all of the essays have been edited from their first draft to avoid overlap with positions taken by others in this volume, or with topics to be taken up in volumes in this series soon to be published. However, each raises major issues that have to be faced as contemporary Christian ethics overcomes its rather stale repetition of quasi-socialist pieties that have governed its thought for decades.

I firmly believe, as I argued in the first essay, that Protestant Christianity must refuse to follow the sectarian impulses that many today advocate. It must not abstract itself from the challenges of modern society and pretend a moral purity by cultivating a precious pietism against the evils of "modern culture," for that denies that the creator God rules over, that Christ is incarnate in, and that the Holy Spirit enlivens the redemptive possibilities of the emerging global

127

tomorrow. What is required beyond the distorting mental maps that block our responsibility to, for, and in the emerging complexities of global civilization, is a theological awareness of the freedom guided by holiness that is at hand, and a renewal of the reforming ethic, now recasting it for a cosmopolitan existence.

As the editor of this volume and the series, I do not intend to argue point for point with the colleagues who have joined in this initial effort, especially since I would have the unfair advantage of being able to both call and play whatever trump I could muster. Thus, I leave most of the debate to the readers and to future conversations with the authors.

It is, however, useful to note that any who decide to join the quest for a reconstructed Christian Social Ethic that is in continuity with the contributions of Protestantism in this area will soon find themselves plunged into debates about monisms and dualisms, red and green, neo-liberalism and neo-conservatives, and into discussions about the virtues and vices of the generations, the role of the world religions in shaping souls and societies, and the responsibilities of the church both to be a public economic critic and to provide an alternative model to those who take market values to be the only ones driving society. Notably, these debates and discussions will be conducted by the use of post-*laissez-faire* and post-Marxist modes of socioeconomic analysis. All the authors here believe that economistic views are simply insufficient for our realities. They can neither interpret nor guide the distinctive complexities of economic life today.

Nor, it turns out, does it help to appeal for more communitarian values unless one can specify the sources, shape, nature, and sustainability of the values and the community, which is what Douglas Meeks attempts to do by drawing more directly on certain motifs in recent liberal Protestant thought and offering a deeper theological underpinning for them. Nevertheless, he too agrees that simply wrapping our minds around the fact that some of the most widely used ways of debating ethical issues are less pertinent to economic life than we have thought is a major gain. We can then debate which decisive ethical, religious, and theological ideas might be better (as I hope to do with him).

At this stage, it makes less difference whether we agree with all of the arguments of all of the authors appearing here (I do not agree with all my colleagues say, nor they with me) than whether we are confronted with the issues that we have to face. On this point, I suspect we agree: we shall have to attend to the social and economic forces forming the values, virtues, and vices of the younger generation, as Peter Berger wisely leads us to recognize. This raises the question of the relationship between the sociology of religion and ethics, and the power of religion and ethics in guiding social developments.

We shall also have to face the transformations of the world religions that invite reconsideration of our views of them and of our own religious traditions, as Dennis McCann points out. This poses the question of the distinctiveness of Christianity in relationship to world religions, and the possible catholicity of the Christian understanding of human nature, social dynamics, and the ethos of civilizational formation.

Surely we shall also have to continue to wrestle with the abiding suspicion of all capitalism and market logic that has been with the study of economics from Aristotle through the saintly ascetics of generations past, which Douglas Meeks articulates in contemporary theological terms and which many secular critics press toward democratic socialism and anti-corporate ecology. Many simply cannot bring themselves to see the modern corporation as a viable community of creative, cooperative association that bears, as much as the school, the political party, or the family, the potential marks of the "household of God" appropriate for its own sphere of action.

Above all, we shall have to recover out of ongoing discussion and debate a profoundly personal and intellectually compelling sense of the holiness and transcendence of God, and on that basis set forth a public theological ethic capable of shaping institutions on a global scale, for it is ever the responsibility of theology in every epoch and every region of the world to provide an articulate view of the deepest and widest inner architecture of civilization, as well as the integrating focus for the soul. Nothing else, indeed, can do that, and we believe that the only fully adequate view of the holy is disclosed by the God whom we know through the created realities of world and Word, through Jesus Christ, and through the power of the Holy Spirit.

In this, we shall need to follow the guiding concerns of my colleagues in this volume: the careful social analysis of operating values that we have in Berger; the reach for a revised catholicity of religious vision and comparative cultural analysis that we see in McCann; and a demand for attention to the significance of teaching and practice in local congregations where theological ethics touches the lives of people in a direct way and thereby, over time, shapes the ethos as a whole, that we find in Meeks.

We invite all who will to join, and further, this effort.

Notes

Notes to Chapter 1

1. The best analysis is Ronald H. Preston, *Confusions in Christian Social Ethics* (London: SCM Press, 1994; Grand Rapids: Wm. B. Eerdmans Publishers, 1995).

2. In my view, some features of these themes are represented in this volume by the essay of M. Douglas Meeks.

3. In this connection, see John M. Staudenmaier, S.J., *Technology's Storytellers* (Cambridge, MA: MIT Press, 1985); Robert H. Nelson, *Reaching for Heaven on Earth: The Theological Meaning of Economics* (Lanham, MD: Rowman and Littlefield, 1991); and Lawrence E. Harrison, *Who Prospers: How Cultural Values Shape Economic and Political Success* (New York: Basic Books, 1992).

4. See Mark Juergensmeyer, *The New Cold War?: Religious Nationalism Confronts the Secular State* (Berkeley: University of California Press, 1994); and Peter van der Veer, *Religious Nationalism: Hindus and Muslims* (Berkeley: University of California Press, 1994).

5. Willy Brandt et al., *North-South: A Program for Survival* (London: Pan Books, 1980; Cambridge, MA: MIT Press, 1981).

6. See, for examples, Rosemary Radford Ruether, *Gaia & God: An Ecofeminist Theology of Earth Healing* (San Francisco: HarperCollins, 1992); and Herman E. Daly and John B. Cobb, Jr., *For the Common Good* (Boston: Beacon Press, 1989). A subsequent volume in the present series, now being written by Thomas Derr, James Nash, and Richard J. Neuhaus, is dedicated to this issue.

7. The recovery of key biblical, classical, historic, world religious, and post-socialist social-scientific treatments of the relation between theology and economic life is the purpose of the 950-page compendium of sources edited by Max L. Stackhouse, Dennis P. McCann, and Shirley L. Roels with Preston N. Williams, *On Moral Business* (Grand Rapids, MI: Wm. B. Eerdmans Publishers, 1995).

8. Simon Kuznetz, *Toward a Theory of Economic Growth* (New York: Norton, 1965); and *The Economic Growth of Nations: Total Output and Production Structure* (Cambridge, MA: Harvard University Press, 1971). I am grateful to Peter Berger, whose writings drew these materials to my attention.

9. Douglass C. North, *Structure and Change in Economic History* (New York: W. W. Norton, 1981).

10. For contrasting views of this issue, see Michael Novak and John W. Cooper, eds., *The Corporation: A Theological Inquiry* (Washington, DC: The American Enterprise Institute, 1981); and James W. Kuhn and Donald W. Shriver, Jr., *Beyond Success: Corporations and Their Critics in the 1990s* (New York: Oxford University Press, 1991).

11. See James W. Skillen, *Recharging the American Experiment: Principled Pluralism for a Genuine Civic Community* (Washington, DC: Center for Public Justice, 1995); and José Casanova, *Public Religions in the Modern World* (Chicago: University of Chicago Press, 1994).

12. This is the topic of the essay by Dennis P. McCann in this volume.

Notes to Chapter 2

1. David Martin, *Tongues of Fire: The Explosion of Protestantism in Latin America* (Oxford and New York: Basil Blackwell, 1990).

2. S. Gordon Redding, *The Spirit of Chinese Capitalism* (Berlin and New York: W. de Gruyter, 1990).

3. Colin Campbell, *The Romantic Ethic and the Spirit of Modern Consumerism* (Oxford and New York: Basil Blackwell, 1987).

4. See Hansfried Kellner and Frank W. Heuberger, eds., *Hidden Technocrats: The New Class and New Capitalism* (New Brunswick, NJ: Transaction Publishers, 1992); and Frank W. Heuberger and Laura L. Nash, eds., *A Fatal Embrace? Assessing Holistic Trends in Human Resources Programs* (New Brunswick, NJ: Transaction Publishers, 1994).

Notes to Chapter 3

1. Ainslie T. Embree, ed., *The Hindu Tradition* (New York: Random House, 1972), 38–39.

2. William Theodore DeBary, trans., *Sources of Indian Tradition* (New York: Columbia University Press, 1958), 16–17.

3. Embree, *The Hindu Tradition*, 82.

4. Ibid., 94.

5. DeBary, *Sources of Indian Tradition*, 231–32.

6. In Peter L. Berger and Hsin-Huang Michael Hsiao, eds., *In Search of an East Asian Development Model* (New Brunswick, NJ: Transaction Books, 1988), 8.

7. In James Finn, ed., *Global Economics and Religion* (New Brunswick, NJ: Transaction Books, 1983), 167–78.

8. Matthews Masayuki Hamabata, *Crested Kimono: Power and Love in the Japanese Business Family* (Ithaca, NY: Cornell University Press, 1990).

9. James M. Fallows, *Looking at the Sun: The Rise of the New East Asian Economic and Political System* (New York: Pantheon Books, 1994).

Notes to Chapter 4

1. A fuller argument can be found in my book *God the Economist: The Doctrine of God and Political Economy* (Minneapolis: Fortress Press, 1989).

2. Some themes here are taken from my "Global Economy and the Globalization of Theological Education," in *The Globalization of Theological Education*, Alice Frazer Evans, Robert A. Evans, and David A. Roozen, eds. (Maryknoll, NY: Orbis Books, 1993).

3. Robert L. Heilbroner, *The Nature and Logic of Capitalism* (New York: W. W. Norton, 1985), 31–32, 141–48, and passim.

4. Karl Polanyi, *The Livelihood of Man* (New York: Academic Press, 1977), 9 and passim.

5. Scott Lash and John Urry, *The End of Organized Capitalism* (Cambridge, MA: Polity, 1987).

6. Robert B. Reich, *The Work of Nations: Preparing Ourselves for 21st Century Capitalism* (New York: Alfred A. Knopf, 1991), 171.

7. Ibid., 268.

8. "Abundant Life for All: Christian Faith and the World Economy Today" (Geneva: World Council of Churches, 1992), 22.

9. Sheldon H. Danziger, Gary D. Sandefur, and Daniel H. Weinberg, *Confronting Poverty: Prescriptions for Change* (Cambridge, MA: Harvard University Press, 1994).

10. William Julius Wilson, *The Truly Disadvantaged: The Inner City, The Underclass and Public Policy* (Chicago: University of Chicago Press, 1987), 8.

11. Richard J. Barnet, *The Lean Years: Politics in the Age of Scarcity* (New York: Simon and Schuster, 1980), and Richard J. Barnet and John Cavanagh, *Global Dreams: Imperial Corporations and the New World Order* (New York: Random House, 1994).

12. Herman E. Daly and John B. Cobb, Jr., *For the Common Good: Redirecting the Economy Toward Community, the Environment, and a Sustainable Future* (Boston: Beacon Press, 1989).

13. Immanuel Levinas, *Totality and Infinity: An Essay on Exteriority*, trans. A. Lingis (Pittsburgh: Duquesne University Press, 1969).

14. Edward Farley, *Good and Evil: Interpreting a Human Condition* (Minneapolis: Fortress Press, 1990).

15. See Meeks, *God the Economist*, 82–89; Michael Ignatieff, *The Needs of Strangers* (New York: Viking Press, 1985); Thomas W. Ogletree, *Hospitality to the Stranger: Dimensions of Moral Understanding* (Philadelphia: Fortress Press, 1985), 35–59; Walter Brueggemann, *Interpretation and Obedience: From Faithful Reading to Faithful Living* (Minneapolis: Fortress Press, 1992), 290–310.

Contributors

Peter L. Berger is Professor of Sociology at Boston University, the Director of the Institute for the Study of Economic Culture, and the author of many articles and books, including *The Capitalist Revolution* (1986), *The Capitalist Spirit: Toward a Religious Ethic of Wealth Creation* (1988), and *A Far Glory* (1992).

Dennis P. McCann is Professor of Business Ethics at DePaul University, the Executive Secretary of the Society of Christian Ethics, and the author of *Christian Realism and Liberation Theology* (1981) and *New Experiment in Democracy: The Challenge for American Catholicism* (1987), among other writings.

M. Douglas Meeks is Professor of Systematic Theology and Dean of Wesley Theological Seminary, and the author of *The Origins of the Theology of Hope* (1974) and *God the Economist: The Doctrine of God and Political Economy* (1989) as well as many other essays.

Max L. Stackhouse is Professor of Christian Ethics at Princeton Theological Seminary, the primary editor of *On Moral Business: Classical and Contemporary Resources for Ethics and Economic Life* (1995), and the author of *Public Theology and Political Economy* (1986, 1991) and *Creeds, Society and Human Rights* (1984).